7 DIMENSIONS *of the* SUPERNATURAL REALM

APOSTLE FREQUENCY REVELATOR

GLOBAL DESTINY PUBLISHING HOUSE

Copyright © 2017 Apostle Frequency Revelator.

All rights reserved. No part of this book may be reproduced, stored in a retrieval system or transmitted in any form or by any means, electronic or mechanical, photographic (photocopying), recording or otherwise, without the written permission of the copyright holder.

ISBN: 9781521758496

The author has made every effort to trace and acknowledge sources, resources and individuals. In the event that any images or information has been incorrectly attributed or credited, the author will be pleased to rectify these omissions at the earliest opportunity.

Scripture quotations are all taken from the Holy Bible, the New King James Version (Authorized Version). First published in 1611. Quoted from the KJV Classic Reference Bible, Copyright © 1983 by The Zondervan Corporation

Published by the Author © Global Destiny Publishing House, No. 17, 5th Street, Sandton, South Africa

Website: www.globaldestinypublishers.co.za

Email: frequency.revelator@gmail.com

Phone: 0027622436745/ 0027785416006/0027797921646

Book layout and cover designed by Mako for Global Destiny Publishing House

OTHER BOOKS PUBLISHED BY APOSTLE FREQUENCY REVELATOR:

How to Become a Kingdom Millionaire

Deeper Revelations of the Anointing

The Realm of Power to Raise the Dead

How to Operate in the Realm of the Miraculous

The Realm of Glory

New Revelations of Faith

Unveiling the Mystery of Miracle Money

The Prophetic Dimension

The Realm of the Spirit: A Divine Revelation of the Supernatural Realm

The Prophetic Move of the Holy Spirit

The Ministry of Angels in the World Today

Throne Room Prayers: The Power of Praying in the Throne Room

Divine Rights and Privileges of a Believer

The Dynamics of God's Word

The Revelation of Jesus Christ

7 Supernatural Dimensions of Financial Prosperity

7 Dimensions of the Supernatural Realm

7 Keys to Unlocking the Supernatural Realm

7 Realms of the Supernatural Dimension

Spiritual Laws and Principles of the Kingdom

Rain of Revelations Daily Devotional Concordance

DEDICATION

This publication remains an exclusive property of Heaven as it has been given birth to by the Holy Ghost in the Throne Room of Heaven. As a product of the fresh breath of God released in the deepest territories of the glory realm, it is geared at propagating deeper revelations of God's Word, Divine presence of the Holy Spirit and Glory from the Throne Room to the extreme ends of the World. Therefore, this book is dedicated to millions of believers, whom through these revelations, shall move and operate in higher realms of the Supernatural, to the glory of God the father!

ACKNOWLEDGEMENTS

This publication is primarily dedicated to the Holy Ghost, who is the author and the finisher of the deep revelations encapsulated in this publication. This insightful, refreshing, profound and biblically sound revelation awakens the believer to the reality of the prophetic move of the Holy Spirit, one of the most important aspects of the God-head. It is chiefly the Holy Ghost who trained me in matters of operating in the deeper realms of the Spirit, hence it is my passion that the reader will see Him throughout the pages of this book and not any man. I would like to express my deep and unparalleled gratitude to my mentors: Dr. Peter Tan of Eagle Vision Ministry for his anointed teachings on the supernatural realm and Pastor Chris the President of the Believers' Love World International Ministry for his deep revelations of the Word of God. I would like to express my deepest and most heartfelt gratitude to my most beautiful and adorable wife Delight Nokuthaba Mpofu who is the love of my life, my life coach and business partner, for having supported me in every way in my ministry as a renowned global author. She is indeed such an amazing blessing that I will forever be grateful to have received from God. I owe a special gratitude specifically to one of my best spiritual sons, Paramjeet Singh Makani from the nation of India, who inspires me a lot through the demonstration of undefinable, uncharted and unrecorded miracles, signs and wonders in this very hour.

I would like to extend my gratitude to my ministry partners for creating such a conducive platform and spiritual climate for me to move in greater depths, higher realms and deeper dimensions of the anointing to shake the nations and touch multitudes around the globe. It is for such a reason that I have been used by God as a vehicle to propagate the new waves of God's anointing to the furthest territories across the globe, to accomplish God's divine plans at such a time as this. Allow me to extend a hand of appreciation to Great men and women of God all around the world who have been an inspiration to me: Dr Yana Johnson (London), Prophetess Nomsa M. Maida of New Breed ministry, Apostle Chris Lord Hills of the Supernatural Church, Dr Franklin (South Africa), Prophet Mathew B. Nuek (Malaysia), Tarsha Howard (USA), Prophetess Menezes (USA) and Prophet Samuel Njagi, for being instrumental in creating a conducive spiritual climate for the birthing forth of the revelations which God has laid in my spirit. Words fail to capture the gratitude I have for my own staff at *Global Destiny Publishing House* (GDP House), who have typified a new type of man coming forth on the earth, rising beyond the confines and dictates of the realm of time, to access higher realms of the Spirit: Further thanks goes to my ministry partners all over the world who have supported me tremendously by demonstrating an unquestionable thirst, perennial hunger and an insatiable appetite to read my books. I command the blessings of the Lord to abundantly marinate every sphere of your life with the rain of the anointing in Jesus Name! Further thanks goes to my siblings namely, Caspa, Kaizer, Target, Keeper, Colleter and Presence Nkomo for their love and support in every way.

- ***Apostle Frequency Revelator***

THE SEVEN DIMENSIONS OF THE SUPERNATURAL REALM

FIRST DIMENSION: The Dimension of Faith

SECOND DIMENSION: The Dimension of The Anointing

THIRD DIMENSION: The Dimension of The Mantle

FOURTH DIMENSION: The Dimension of The Presence

FIFTH DIMENSION: The Dimension of the Miraculous

SIXTH DIMENSION: The Dimension of Glory

SEVENTH DIMENSION: The God Dimension: The Love Dimension

CONTENTS

PREFACE

AN INTRODUCTORY PERSPECTIVE TO THE SEVEN DIMENSIONS OF THE SUPERNATURAL REALM

In this publication, Apostle Frequency Revelator explores the divine revelation of the **7 Universal dimensions of the supernatural realm** which believers can progress through in their spiritual journey or voyage of exploration of the greater depths of the spirit realm. It is worth exploring the divine truth that Faith is the *first dimension* of the supernatural realm, the Anointing is the *second dimension* and the Mantle is the *third dimension.* So, in order to tap into the higher realms of supernatural, one has to step out or be catapulted from the realm of faith (*first dimension*) through the realm of the anointing (*second dimension*) into the realm of the mantle (*third dimension*). The grand entrance into the realm of the anointing is through faith. Faith is the ever empowering awareness of the invisible world and its realities. Faith is the currency of Heaven and functions as an antenna whose frequency is being tuned to the spiritual waves that come directly from the Throne room of Heaven. Although faith is a lower plane in the realm of God and a starting point for all humanity endeavouring to reach the realm of eternity, faith is what introduces you to the anointing and accentuates an avenue for the glory of God to be manifested. The anointing is the divine impartation of God's supernatural abilities and traits upon an available and yielded vessel in order to undertake delegated divine tasks efficiently and effectively. The solidification and build-up of the anointing will usher you into another higher dimension called the *mantle,* which is an emblem of God's manifest presence in the natural realm and functions as a spiritual covering that rests upon an individual in order to exercise a heightened degree of authority or dominion over a territory.

The Presence is the *fourth dimension* of the supernatural, the Miraculous is the *fifth dimension* and the Glory is the *sixth dimension* while Love is the *7th and highest dimension*, coined as the *God Dimension.* As we continue to progress heavenward in the spirit realm, you can be catapulted from the presence (*Fourth Dimension*), into the miraculous arena (*fifth dimension*) and from the miraculous domain into the Glory realm until you are thrust into the (Love) God dimension which is the 7th and highest Dimension of the supernatural. The presence represents a radiation or refection of God's glory. It is the manifest touch that comes when the glory of God is radiated in a particular place. The presence is not the glory but the radiation or refection of that glory. It is a signal that God is in the house. Basically, the anointing of God is a manifestation of the power of God while the glory of God is a manifestation of His attributes. However, the power of God and the presence of God are inseparable because God does not demonstrate His power without His presence. On the other hand, the miraculous is an incredible happening, occurrence or unusual manifestation that takes place in the natural realm as a result of a sudden divine intervention of God in the affairs of humanity to the extent that it cannot be fathomed or comprehended by human reasoning and intellectual ability. It is an instantaneous manifestation of God's tangible and visible supernatural power in the normal course of an individual's life, with a consequence of defying the natural laws of time, space and matter.

The glory is a tangible and visible supernatural manifestation of the fullness or totality of God from the realm of the spirit into the realm of the physical. This implies that the glory is God in His totality or state of perfection and completeness. It is the intrinsic essence of who God is characterised or manifested by His nature, character, being, attributes or virtues. This implies that the glory is the nature of God and an exact representation or extension of his being. It proceeds from him; it is part of His being. It could also be described as the divine impartation and revelation of the substance, heaviness, imminence, supremacy of the transcending presence of God in the affairs of humanity. While the anointing is given to an individual for service to complete specific tasks, the glory is given for elevation or promotion in the spirit. The glory comes as a result of one having completed successfully the delegated divine tasks. Hence, the anointing is what breeds the glory because the anointing causes one to execute tasks and brings them to perfect completion which would then entitle one to be in a position to receive the glory. In other words, the anointing lays a fertile ground for the glory of God to be revealed. The anointing is given to bring the glory of God into manifestation. You get to see the glory of God through the anointing because the anointing is what connects you to the glory of God. It lays a groundwork or preparation platform for the glory to be revealed or manifested. God's presence and power are resident in the anointing, hence any man of God who taps into the realm of the anointing and manifests miracles, signs and wonders ushers the glory of God on the scene. In this case, the anointing reveals or manifests the glory of God.

In our journey in the spirit dimension, there is a realm which a man can be catapulted into which marks the highest level of spiritual contact with God. At that level of life, one is not chasing after any needs but rather after the heart of God. It is called the *seventh dimension.* That realm is the realm of love. It is a realm of perfection. It is a dimension in which God Himself lives, breathes and operates. That is a realm in which when catapulted into, you lose your own self-consciousness and begins to think as God thinks, talk as God talks, see as God sees and consequently view all things from God's perspective. In other words, in that realm where you begin to pour out the heart of God into every situation that you encounter. In that realm, everything is complete and perfect. Sickness, pain and death cannot operate in that realm. It is the most powerful than any other dimension which man can ever function in this world.

THE 7 RDIMENSIONS OF THE SUPERNATURAL REALM ARE AS FOLLOWS:

1. **FIRST DIMENSION: The Dimension of Faith**

2. **SECOND DIMENSION: The Dimension of The Anointing**

3. **THIRD DIMENSION: The Dimension of The Mantle**

4. **FOURTH DIMENSION: The Dimension of The Presence**

5. **FIFTH DIMENSION: The Dimension of the Miraculous**

6. **SIXTH DIMENSION: The Dimension of Glory**

7. **SEVENTH DIMENSION: The God Dimension: The Love Dimension**

THE DIVINE REVELATION OF SEVEN DIMENSIONS OF THE SUPERNATURAL REALM

It is worth exploring the divine truth that faith is the *first dimension* of the supernatural realm, the anointing is the *second dimension* and the glory is the *sixth dimension.* So, in order to tap into the higher realms of glory, one has to step out or be catapulted from the realm of faith (*first dimension*) through the realm of the anointing (*second dimension*) into the realm of the mantle (*third dimension*) until one is catapulted to the realm of glory (*Sixth dimension*). Other dimensions include prior to reaching the dimension of glory are the presence (*Fourth Dimension*), the miraculous (*fifth dimension*) until one is catapulted to the God dimension which is the 7th highest Dimension. The grand entrance into the realm of glory is through faith. Faith is the ever empowering awareness of the invisible world and its realities. Faith is the antenna whose frequency is being tuned to the spiritual waves that come directly from the throne room of Heaven. Although faith is a lower plane in the realm of God and a starting point for all humanity endeavouring to reach the realm of eternity, faith is what introduces you to the glory and accentuates an avenue for the glory of God to be revealed.

The greater truth is that faith is a currency of Heaven. You need faith to trade with God at His level and to withdraw from the resourcefulness of His glory. Faith is the time zone in which God dwells. It is, it was, and it is to come. Faith is a higher law than time and it permits us to live, and operate, in that higher law. Through faith, we can access out of time into the eternal. Therefore, faith is the bridge, or passageway, the connection between time or eternity. Without faith the apprehension of an entrance into the eternal realm by the Spirit would not be possible. We are often crises-oriented, meaning that we fail to perceive the Glory of God because we have conformed to the sense realm in which our crises exists. This type of perception or complex makes what we are actually seeing complicated with intellectualism and fact, not truth.

The question you are probably asking yourself is: *How did the concept of faith come about? Surely the first man Adam did not need faith to reach out to God!* The truth is that following the fall of man in the Garden of Eden, God has always had problems in dealing with humanity, in that He is reaching from the eternal realm into a limited realm of time and space. In this respect He speaks a language we cannot understand. We are unable to relate to eternity from within a time realm. How could this gap be bridged? It was up to God to take the initiative and solve this problem of communication failure. It would require a key to decode His thoughts, something that would work in both realms. It had to be a valid medium of exchange in the realm of eternity and the realm of time. Therefore, He provided a medium of exchange, valid in Heaven and on earth when He gave us faith.

Faith is the currency, or gold standard, of the eternal realm, and also an honoured currency, or standard, in the earth. God had to give man faith in order to elevate him above the constraints of time, space and matter so that man could have an intelligent relationship with His Creator. The fallen mind of man cannot understand the eternal realm, nor grasp the fact that he was created for a higher dimension than what time, space and matter would determine for him. The human mind can hardly conceive that he has been given the key to subdue and change his predetermined boundaries set by time and space. The key is faith. God gave us the gift of faith to open the prison door of time and escape, and freely access His glorious realm. The door swings both ways, giving us access to Him, and God direct access to us, without the limitations of doubt. Once the faith key is turned in the lock of time, nothing is impossible to man. He can then freely access the treasures of His loving Father. Unencumbered by the weight of disbelief, we can then enter freely into His presence. We no longer doubt what God said He would do or when He said he would do it. Time is no threat to such a one. This thrills God, as He finds access to such a heart and mind and for that one, nothing shall be impossible in the supernatural dimension of glory.

The glory makes it easy for one to function in the realm of the anointing. As much as the anointing connects us to the glory of God, it must be understood that in some cases operating and moving in the anointing is dependent on the degree of the glory present. Remember that the *anointing is God's ability imparted upon a vessel but the glory is God himself doing His work* hence, when God manifests His glory in a particular area, the extent to which we can manifest that glory through the anointing is dependent on the measure of the glory that is manifested. We should therefore learn to be sensitive to the varying levels of the glory of manifested if ever we want to move in greater dimension of the anointing. According to the level of God's glory manifested, we can function easily in the anointing. Sometimes in a meeting, everyone's concentration is so perfectly upon the attributes of God, that the glory of God comes into manifestation. When the glory of God is in manifestation, it is easier to function in the ministerial anointing. Do not function beyond the level of God's glory manifested. Each meeting, for various reasons has a different degree of manifested glory and anointing. The realm of glory is what rules or governs the realm of the anointing and not vice versa. There is a limitation for the functions of an anointing set by the manifested glory in each meeting although in the fivefold calling we may actually carry a greater anointing than we are allowed to manifest at that time.

The realm of Glory enables us to move, live and function in both the realm of the spirit and the realm of the natural at the same time. It is only possible through the glory of God to function in both the spiritual world and the natural world concurrently. Although faith connects us to the spirit realm, it is the glory of God that causes us to operate freely in both realms of existence. Faith is a spiritual connection but when the glory comes, it gives way. That is why man is allowed to use faith in the absence of the glory but when the glory comes, man does not need faith to operate in the glory because it is God Himself doing His own work. It is worth exploring the divine truth that man's original state was void of circumstance as we know it because of the Glory in which he lived in the little Heavenly realm on earth called *Eden*. Eden was an epitome of a manifestation of *Heaven on earth*. One of the meanings of the word "*Eden*" in Hebrew is "*a moment in time*". When God made man, He placed him in one of these moments in time. In that moment in time, he could easily switch between the two realms of existence. Before the fall, Adam operated easily in both realms of existence. He could move into the spirit realm and talk to God and then move back to the natural realm to interact with his animals. Moving from the natural realm into the spiritual realm was like moving from his bedroom into the living room. Enoch is another quintessential example of a man of two realms, by faith living in the unseen. He operated so much in both realms of the existence to the extent that he permanently disappeared into the other world, the eternal one.

Jesus also demonstrated the spiritual reality of living in the two realms of existence at the same time when He declared in prophetic language in John 3:13 that, "*No one has been to Heaven, except the Son of man which is in heaven*".

The question you are probably asking yourself is: How can Jesus be in Heaven and on earth at the same time? It's because of the life in the glory. It is the glory that enables man to see in the spirit and natural realm at the same time as in an open vision. Although Jesus had a ministry to accomplish on earth at that time, He simultaneously operated in the heavenly realm of glory from which He came and that is why miracles and signs and wonders were mightily demonstrated through His hands. Elijah also functioned in both realms, this why he was able to control the economy of heaven, by shutting and opening it at his own discretion. His popular statement of address: "*I stand in the presence of God*", depicts this dual role which he played across both realms. We have also been catapulted into this realm because the Bible says *we are seated with Christ in the heavenly places.* That means while we walk and work in this earth, our positions of authority, governance and offices are in the spirit realm and as we operate in that realm, we are able to influence activities of heaven and earth. That is why Bible says *whatever we bind on earth shall be bound in heaven.* Why? Because we operate in the heavenly realm of glory which governs both heaven and earth, hence whatever we decree in that realm, heaven is bound to respond with an answer.

Paul, the apostle, said there were times he was *"between and betwixt"*. In other words, he seemed to be in and out of both the spiritual and natural worlds at the same time. He could not tell if it was his spirit only or his body and spirit were taken to the third heaven to see things, many of which he was not allowed to describe. The Apostle Paul speaks in 2 Corinthians 12:1-4 of being caught up to the third Heaven:

> *"It is not expedient for me doubtless to glory. I will come to visions and revelations of the Lord. I knew a man in Christ above fourteen years ago, (whether in the body, I cannot tell; or whether out of the body, I cannot tell: God knoweth;) such an one caught up to the third heaven. And I knew such a man, (whether in the body, or out of the body, I cannot tell: God knoweth;) How that he was caught up into paradise, and heard unspeakable words, which it is not lawful for a man to utter.*

In the context of the above-mentioned scripture, the phrase, "*Caught up*" implies being catapulted into a higher realm of glory". In other words, Paul was simultaneously caught up into the Glory and into the future. Allegorically speaking, the future is up, not somewhere before us in this earthly time zone. While man has a tendency to think horizontally, God manifests vertically, the impact of which issues out horizontally. Our future is in the Glory, where everything comes from. Paul stepped into the world that simultaneously exists with the eternal, or supernatural. As we enter into the *Glory cloud,* we also can experience what the Apostle Paul did. What an exciting possibility! To substantiate this divine truth with reference to experiential evidence, in my person experience in ministry, I have been to Heaven, scripturally referred to as "*being caught up in the spirit*", walked the streets of gold, stood in the Throne room, seen Jesus, talked to angels and heard mysteries which are not part of the vocabulary of modern man, then came back to the natural realm, taught the masses the deep revelations of Heaven and mightily demonstrated the power of God through miracles signs and wonders. This was only possible because of the atmosphere of glory which enabled me to easily swift between Heaven and earth.

In the word of God, three key dimensions of the supernatural realm are revealed, namely *faith,* the *anointing* and the *glory*. Likewise, there are three feasts that correspondingly represent the *three realms* of the supernatural namely, the *Feast of Passover*, the *Feast of Pentecost* and the *Feast of Tabernacles*. Passover symbolises faith, Pentecost symbolises the *anointing* and Tabernacles symbolises the *glory*. The truth is that you cannot understand the glory if you don't first understand *anointing* and you cannot understand the anointing if you don't have faith to catapult you into that higher dimension. The battle many preachers always have is introducing people into the glory of God. Faith is a voluntary act based on our knowledge or conviction. Faith is the first dimension into the supernatural. It is the legal entry into the invisible or supernatural realm. It is the key to operate and work in the eternal realm. It is the ability of the believer to believe something that is unreasonable. Faith is NOW and requires a revelation from now. You cannot have a present faith without a present revelation. We don't see a heightened degree of miracles today in the church because miracles occur in the NOW, not yesterday. Most of the decisions we make are based on time, not on faith. If it is not now, it is not faith. Faith is the prerequisite to enter into the glory. Many people want to enter the glory but don't even know what faith is. In essence, it is the substance of the spiritual world. When Jesus heard that, He said, "*This sickness is not unto death, but for the glory of God, that the Son of God may be glorified through it.*"(John 11:4). Martha wanted to enter into the glory for Jesus to raise Lazarus from the dead but Jesus corrected her faith first. This is evidenced by His statement, *"Didn't I tell you that you must believe to see the glory of God?"* That means believing is what introduces us to the realm of glory. The glory of God is not revealed to everybody but only to those who would step into that dimension through faith. Faith has been given to each and every one of us by measure. You must first believe in order to see the glory of God. Entering in His glory is a reward of your faith; it is His greatest reward. Faith is supernatural but we have reduced it to something natural. We have reduced it to optimism and motivational messages. But when you preach faith, the most amazing miracles take place because it is NOW from a present revelation.

The next dimension (*Second dimension*) of the supernatural that introduces us into the realm of glory is *the anointing*. The anointing is an aspect of the supernatural power of God that empowers us to fulfil the purpose and calling here on earth. It is one of the aspects of His power working through us. It has been given to each and every one of us by measure. We need each other because we have measures that others don't have, and vice versa. But to each one of us grace was given according to the measure of Christ's gift. (Ephesians 4:7). We don't have it all in ourselves; we need each other. Anointing is the power of God working through you. It is the seal in your spirit you to experience the glory. In Him you also trusted, after you heard the word of truth, the gospel of your salvation; in whom also, having believed, you were sealed with the Holy Spirit of promise, (Ephesians 1:13). The anointing was given to us for the earth. There are no blind, deaf or sick people in heaven. There are none who are broken hearted and oppressed. You do not need anointing in heaven; it is for the earth. It is not for your pride or for your fame. God wants to release His anointing to humble people who love His people. If you are a pastor and you wanted to die with that mantle, it is best if you start transferring it on the next generation.

"The Spirit of the LORD is upon Me, Because He has anointed Me to preach the gospel to the poor; He has sent Me to heal the broken hearted, to proclaim liberty to the captives and recovery of sight to the blind, to set at liberty those who are oppressed (Luke 4:18).

God give us anointing because we all fell short of the glory of God (Romans 3:23). Man was under the glory, not the anointing, before sin and so God gave us anointing so that we are able to move in the supernatural realm. In other words, after falling short of the glory of God (Romans 3:23), God gave man the anointing as a back-up.

The next dimension into the supernatural realm is the glory. The glory is the third dimension. The glory of God is the manifested presence of God Himself. It is the realm of eternity. It is eternity revealed, without limits or restrictions. It is the atmosphere of God Himself. Each manifestation is from the nature and character of God Himself. It is not His power operating through us, but rather it is God Himself doing His own works. We have limited God because we think He has to do His works through a human being. While this is true in the anointing and in faith, in His glory He works by His own initiative. It is beyond your measure of faith and anointing. It is God Himself, in all of His attributes and majesty. When God performs a miracle in you without you having the faith to believe for it or the anointing to manifest it, it is God Himself touching you directly. I had been in meetings where, without even touching anyone, miracle after miracle begins taking place. It had nothing to do with people's faith, anointing or gifts but the glory of God!

CHAPTER ONE

FIRST DIMENSION:

THE DIMENSION OF FAITH

Have you ever wondered why a multitude of people claim to have prayed, fasted and done everything they know best but their situations and circumstances haven't changed?. Have you ever given yourself a moment to think about dozens of believers who are entangled in a morass of debilitating poverty, lack, and limitation yet they claim to believe God? Have you ever wondered why some people have even gone to the extent of being discouraged in their Christian walk because their prayers were not answered? The answer to all the above scenarios is not in lack of power, wisdom or prayer but it is simply *an issue of lack of faith.* Many of God's people pray, fast, cry, sow seeds, confess scriptures and still experience frustration and even tragedies in their finances, health, jobs, marriages and businesses because they haven't learnt how to properly and correctly exercise their faith and make it work. It is an irrefutable fact that an element which is regarded as absolutely essential to the development of the Christian life is *the quality of faith.* Faith is what makes a Christian different from a non-Christian and a successful Christian from a struggling one. This is because faith is what sets all other spiritual laws in motion hence you might have done everything which you think should be done and applied every spiritual law and principle but if you don't have faith, all those laws and things you are believing God for will not work out for you.

The greater truth is that faith lays an unshakable foundation upon which other spiritual laws and principles are laid. For example, if you just religiously make beggarly prayers without faith, your prayers won't work, if you give grudgingly without faith, your giving is not counted for anything in the spirit and if you fast, without faith, it would just be like you are on a hunger strike and no significant impact would be made in the realm of the spirit. This is because faith is *the presiding currency of Heaven* and for anything to be legalized or for any transaction to be deemed legal between heaven and earth, it must have been done through faith. Faith is a license that legally ordains any movement, transference or release of blessings between heaven and earth hence no man can receive anything from heaven without faith. As much as no man can live on earth without oxygen, no man can live or operate in the spirit realm without faith. As oxygen is to a human body, so is faith to a man in the spirit. In the spirit, virtually everything revolves around *the phenomenon of faith.* Faith is the most integral and fundamental aspect of a successful Christian life. Without faith, it is impossible to please God because firstly, faith is a realm in which God lives, operates and functions. A man who operates in faith functions at the level and class as God. Secondly, faith is the spiritual language which God speaks, hence, if you cannot please Him by speaking His language, then you cannot make any significant impact in the spirit realm. Therefore you can only please God if you talk as God talks, see as God sees, and acts as God acts and this is only possible through faith.

However, it is of paramount significance to unveil the truth that a multitude of books have been written on faith yet this subject remains a mystery and the most misunderstood and misinterpreted in the Christian fraternity. The reality is that, of the innumerable gifts with which God has bestowed upon humanity, faith is the greatest gift that is often overlooked or misunderstood, yet it is the most critical in a Christian life since our relationship with God is grossly dependent on it. Moreover, hundreds of thousands of sermons preach about faith and millions of words discuss faith yet it still remains a hazy, mysterious and unfathomable phenomenon. Although faith is a widely discussed subject in Charismatic Christian faith, what is lacking is the ingredient of revelation of what faith is, how it operates, how to practically exercise or demonstrate it as well as the spiritual principles and laws that governs its operation. The truth of the matter is that *faith* is greatly misunderstood as there are many peculiar ideas of what it is. Casual readers of the word do not have an in-depth understanding and revelation of what exactly faith is except the elementary truth that *it is a substance of things hoped for.* As a consequence, the concept of faith has been diluted, misinterpreted or rather misconstrued by bad theology. John Wesley once said that, *"The devil has given the Church a substitute for faith; one that looks and sounds so much like faith that few people can tell the difference. This substitute is called "mental assent."*

Many people read God's Word and agree that it is true, but they are agreeing only with their minds. And that is not what gets the job done. It is heart faith that receives from God. Memorizing scriptures on faith will not get the job done either except to take that word into your spirit through constant *imagination, meditation, confession and then take a practical step of action.* Therefore, this writing is a Holy Ghost breathing that centers on accurately and comprehensively unveiling the mystery of what faith is, what faith is not, as well as how to practically exercise it to produce results of success in every sphere of your life.

It is a typical situation across the wide spectrum of Christian faith that a multitude of people have prayed, fasted and exercised their faith in every sphere of human endeavour but have not yet seen any positive results of their confession because they have mistaken their exercise of faith for presumption, confidence, optimism or hope. This writing therefore provides a solution, answer and a practical model that gives divine correction and guidance of what real, genuine faith is so that people can exercise faith in the right way in order to produce positive results. It clarifies first of all, what faith is not since the whole concept of faith is one of the most misunderstood ideas not only by the world but by the church itself. Faith, for instance, is not positive thinking; that is something quite different. Faith is not hoping for the best either. Hoping that everything will turn out all right is nit faith at all. Faith is not a feeling of optimism. Faith is none of these things, though all of them have been identified by multitudes of believers as faith.

Moreover, a multitude of believers across the globe only know the elementary truth of faith *as the substance of things hoped for and the evidence of things not seen* and their revelation just ends there. They never go beyond this level to seek an in-depth revelation of how faith operates. As a result, they are not experiencing humongous blessings from heaven because their level of their faith is too low for the full blessings of the Lord to be manifested in their lives. As a matter of faith, many people have not been able to receive answers to their prayers because their faith level is so low that they are not making any significant impact in the spirit realm. The principle that *without faith it is impossible to please God infers that without faith it is impossible to receive from God* because receiving from God is an evidence of having pleased Him. The truth is that God blesses a man *according to the measure of faith* he has and if God gives you something beyond the level of your faith, then it might suffocate you. It must therefore be expressly understood that the level of blessings which a man can receive from God is directly proportional or tantamount to the level of faith he is operating at. Therefore, the greater the faith, the greater the blessings and on the other side of the coin, the lower the faith, the lesser the blessing.

Prophetically speaking, the reading of this book is therefore such an impulse that shall put the springs of faith into your spirit and catapult you to higher realms of power, blessings, breakthrough and promotion. Therefore if you want promotion, prosperity, healing, a humongous instantaneous breakthrough, or millions of heaven's wealth to manifests speedily in your life than you have ever dreamed possible, then continue to marinate your spirit with a flood of revelations encapsulated in this book. This book provides a solution to a myriad of problems and questions that for ages have remained unanswered. It gives accurate answers as to why your faith did not work before, why you did not receive answers to your prayers and why you did not receive the dimension of blessings which you believed God for. However, if your faith did not work before, it is not too late. Following the spiritual principles of faith unveiled in this writing, you can now go back and exercise your faith again, with revelation knowledge and you will be thrilled at how at the account of your faith God shall cause humongous blessings to manifest speedily in measures you have never dreamt of before. Prophetically speaking, following the reading of this book, many people are going to receive alarming breakthroughs in their ministry, families, career and business as a result of studying and applying practical principles of faith unveiled in this writing. While you are still reading, the faith level in your spirit will be so impacted such that you cannot but rise higher.

THE ESSENCE OF FAITH

The word faith comes from a Latin word *fidere*, which means to trust, believe in something. Faith has been defined as an "*unquestioning belief* " in God. Faith generally means having a strong conviction, deep trust, reliance upon, or loyalty to God. In the Old Testament the Hebrew word for faith is *emuwn* which means to trust, or have faith. In the New Testament the Greek word for faith is *pistis*, which means to trust, believe, have faith or rely upon. The biblical definition of real faith is found in the book of Hebrews. This popular portion of the Scripture plainly state that "faith is the *substance* of things hoped for, and the *evidence* of things not [yet] seen" (Hebrews 11:1). Substance means assurance, realization, something like a title or deed to a house or piece of property. Evidence entails proof. The author of Hebrews states *"By faith we understand that the worlds were formed by the word [command] of God, so that the things that are seen [the creation] were not made of things that are visible"* (Hebrews 11:3). *Real* faith rests on *solid proof*—not just feelings, conjecture or wishful thinking. The modern notion that faith doesn't rest on proof actually*undermines* the real faith that Scripture talks about.

However, it is of paramount significance to highlight in this section the divine truth that the subject of faith can be comprehensively examined and studied from different perspectives. The reality is that only confining our definition of faith as *a substance of things hoped for* is just a basic, elementary truth hence believers are cautiously advised to go beyond that basic revelation to dissect the subject of faith in detail because grabbing just one slice of the word and running with it it's not what gets the job done. It is a thorough cross referencing and examination of scriptures coupled with an optimum integration of both theoretical and practical scenarios in God's word that makes a difference. Therefore in the context of this revelation, defining faith from such a holistic perspective is meant to reinforce a significant level of the concept. Faith is therefore defined as a *spiritual substance, state of being, evidence, an assurance, title deed, a rebuttal force or simply a language of the spirit.*

FAITH IS A SPIRITUAL SUBSTANCE

Unknown to many people, faith has a *spiritual materiality*. In other words, it is a product of divine orchestration in the spirit realm hence it can be best described as a *spiritual substance.* It is a *substance* in the sense that it is tangible, real and substantial. To substantiate this revelation with reference to scriptural evidence, the Bible says in Hebrews 11:1 that,

Now faith is the **substance** *of things hoped for, the conviction of things not seen.*

In the context of the above scripture, the word substance implies that, like any other substance in the natural realm, faith has properties of weight, mass, and density hence it can be measured, touched, and even weighed. We therefore need to get that into our consciousness the reality that there is such a thing as a *spiritual substance*. From a scientific point of view, the word substance means a matter, something heavy, tangible, see able and feel able, something that can be touched. By the same token, faith is a tangible spiritual substance. *Faith is a tangible, visible spiritual substance.* That means faith can be touched, seem, felt and experienced. Spiritually speaking, the word "*substance*" is *hypostasis*, which is the word you use when you want to talk about something that is concrete and physical. So to call faith the substance "of things hoped for" is to say that people with faith live as though their hopes have been substantiated in front of them, which is of course a paradox because hope stops being just hope when it is substantiated into reality. In the spirit realm, everything that leaves heaven to earth is sent forth as a tangible spiritual substance that has value. Just as our physical eyesight is the sense that gives us evidence of the material world, faith is the «*sense*" that gives us evidence of the invisible, spiritual world. If you have hope for anything, faith is what gives it substance. Faith gives you every reason to affirm something is yours before you see it with your physical eyes. Why? Faith is the substance of things hoped for; it calls real those things that are not physically observable. It calls them done NOW!

As much as there are natural substances, there are also spiritual substances. The spirit world has its own material form for example angels have a form and when God created angels, He took spiritual substances from the spirit realm and brought it together. Later when God created man, He created him in a different realm with a spiritual ability. The bible also talks about the food of angels as a spiritual substance and in Psalms; it says that the manna that the Israelites ate was angels' food. In other words, it was transformed into a physical world so that the physical man can eat it and survive. For 40 years the whole nation of Israel survived on manna from heaven and that manna provided all the protein, carbohydrates, vitamins and minerals that they needed. It is remarkable that the spiritual substance can become a physical substance and provide everything that the physical world could have provided. Did the angels eat this manna too? Yes they did; that is why it is called in the book of Psalms angels' food.. However, faith is not the only spiritual substance. Grace is a spiritual substance. Glory is a spiritual substance. A lot of the gifts of God are impartations of spiritual substances. Based on this realisation, it is therefore unequivocally evident that there is a substance that is very real in the spirit realm. Philosophically speaking, everything that leaves heaven to earth comes as a spiritual substance from the spirit world.

By the same token, Faith is a spiritual substance. The bible further declares in Hebrews 11:6 that,

> *Without faith it is impossible to please God. For whoever would draw near to God must believe that He exists and He rewards those who seek Him.*

In our earlier reference to (Hebrews 11:3), the bible says that faith is a substance and now it says without faith it is impossible to please Him. In a view to enhance a significant level of understanding of this spiritual reality, I want to use that expression and replace the word *"faith"* with the word *"spiritual substance"* in verse 6 so that i can show you how it can sound different. It now reads, without *spiritual substance* it is impossible to please Him. For he who comes to God must believe that He exists in the realm of the spirit and He is a rewarder of those who diligently seek Him. Can you see the impact of that statement now? Without spiritual substance it is impossible to please Him. The first was faith is a spiritual substance. Then we bring it further in verse 6 without the spiritual substance it is impossible to please God. Since it says without faith it is impossible to please God and faith is a spiritual substance. You just replace those words and you find that without spiritual substance it is impossible to please God. And we have verse 6 without spiritual substance it is impossible to please God. There must be something imparted from God into our life that enables us to please Him, to do that which He wants us to do. Without that spiritual substance nothing can happen that could be pleasing to God.

> *One peculiar characteristic of the spirit world affecting our life is not just by believing something. There must be some real impartation of a spiritual substance that comes into our life.*

It is therefore undeniably evident that everything in the spirit world is the spiritual substance. And everything that we receive from God comes in a form of spiritual substances. If you receive wisdom from God, God imparts some real substances into your spirit. Now I know He could give spiritual substances in measures. And the spirit of God's presence in our life is also a sort of spiritual substances coming into our life. We have to accept the fact that the anointing of God is a spiritual substance. The Holy Spirit is a person but the anointing of God, which comes from the Holy Spirit, and the *dunamis* of God is a spiritual substance. The spiritual attributes of wisdom, knowledge, power, authority, love, peace, joy, self-control, meekness, can be viewed as spiritual substances. The anointing of God is a substance of God. The power of the Holy Spirit is a substance of God. Let me redefine the whole system. Practically everything in the spirit world is a substance. You may have never viewed these attributes as substances before. But I want you to know that they are substances. It's a different question when you talk about how the substance is imparted and what actually happens. You have never thought of humility or meekness as a substance. And yet we know that there are different degrees of humility. Many people don't think of wisdom as a substance. But it is a substance. Therefor faith is a spiritual substance that can be imparted into our spirit so that we are able to function in the realm of God to please Him.

"Faith is not just believing or having a strong spiritual conviction about something but taking the right steps or action, at the right time, in the right place to produce results of what the word of God talks about"

It is a typical scenario in many Christian cycles that a multitude of people actually mistake faith for believing. In essence, they are believing instead of expressing faith. There is a difference between faith and believing. Before I could clarify the difference between these two concepts, let me first start by clarifying their similarities. The relationship between believing and faith is that believing lays a foundation of faith because you cannot have faith on what you don't believe in. If you don't believe on something, then it becomes practically impossible to exercise faith for it. For example if one does not believe in God, then he cannot exercise faith to receive from him. It therefore follows that believing lays a conducive ground and a platform upon which faith could be exercised. In essence, *belief is an expression and an integral aspect of faith.* Believing is therefore that ingredient, or prerequisite that is required for one to jump start his faith. The bible declares in Romans 10:17 that,

Faith comes from hearing and hearing the word of God.

This implies that it takes a step of faith to hear the word but it also takes believing to take you to a place where you can hear the word. That means you need to believe first in the word before you could take a practical step to get to a place where you could hear it being preached or ministered.

However, while faith and believing have been labelled by many biblical scholars and theologians as intertwined processes with overlapping spheres of influence, in essence, they are not the same. In actual fact, there is a significant difference between faith and believing. To believe means to be in a state of expectancy where you envision in your spirit a positive outcome in every situation. Believing refers to the spiritual act of having trust or total dependence on something but faith is an evidence of unseen realities. While both acts are expressions of the human spirit, believing focuses on having a strong spiritual conviction about a given spiritual phenomenon while faith a tangible spiritual substance accompanied by action. Belief holds on to something unseen but faith sees into the spirit. Faith has eyes; it moves, touches and sees in the spirit while belief is only based on the unseen.

The greater truth is that believing is not faith and faith is not believing. To believe is different from having faith. Philosophically speaking, just as a dog is not a cat and a cat is not a dog, believing is not faith and faith is not believing. However, belief and faith work together. Believing writes the digits on the cheque but it is faith that cashes the cheque. Believing will make you die with a good attitude. On its own believing writes a smile on your face whilst the ship is sinking. Faith on the other hand keeps the boat afloat and gives you a good attitude. Though belief is the starting point of faith, it will not change the circumstances of your life. It is faith that changes your circumstances. You cannot get results in life by just believing that you will receive blessings. Believing is a noun – Faith is a doing word. Faith is a verb and a verb is an act. In their original contexts, the Greek word for believing is '*dechomai*' meaning passive receiving while the Greek word for Faith is "*lambano*" meaning seizing as if by military force. You need to act upon that which you believe. Faith is acting upon what you believe. To cement this revelation with reference to simple example, if you go into your kitchen and put a pot full of water on the stove and raise up your hands and say "*I really believe that if I put the stove ON, this water in the pot will boil*". I tell you the truth; you will be there until you die unless you put your finger on the 'ON' button for the water to boil. Though your believing might be very right, it will not make the water boil if the 'ON' button needed to heat up the stove is not pressed. This implies that you need to act upon what you believe for it to work. Now let me quickly reiterate here that there's a difference between faith and believing. Many people don't understand that difference. To enhance a significant understanding of this revelation, let me illustrate it with reference to a practical example. A man who's suffering from a form of sickness might cry, "*Oh God, I believe! Oh God, I really know You can do it.* Do it *for me today! Heal me Lord!*" He doesn't realize it but that's not faith. All he's doing is expressing his believing. That fellow might be discouraged and unhappy if he doesn't receive healing, because he'll think to himself, "*If I've ever had faith in my life that was one time I had faith!*" He'll be wondering, "*Oh God, why didn't I receive*?" not knowing that what he had was not faith at all.

The greater truth is that believing is a state or attitude of the heart while faith is a proclamation of the spirit because the bible says if you believe with your heart and confess with your mouth that Jesus is Lord, then you are saved (Romans 10:9). This implies that believing is a state of the heart and although it lays a strong foundation upon which one's faith can be built, it does not constitute faith because it lacks action, veracity of evidence and substantiation. Believing is done in the heart and ends there, yet faith is proven with an outward action. *Without that action on the outside there is no faith*. What will be present is '*believing*' and believing ends in the heart. It is not faith for it has no action attached to it. It ends in the heart. Romans 10:10 says,

For it is with the heart man believeth.

When the believing is done in the heart you need to act upon it for it to be faith, otherwise it will simply be believing and that will not change your circumstances. Believing is only the starting point and if all you do is believe in your heart but do nothing about what you believe, then there will be no faith. In so saying *dechomai* is of the heart and ends there but *lambano* comes out of the heart to perform in the natural what has been dechomaid through the heart.

This implies that it is possible for one to believe something even without saying anything but it is not possible to have faith and keep quiet about it because faith is a proclamation or speaking the word of God in a particular situation with intent to effect change or bring forth results. Believing is a silent force but faith is a vocal expression of what one believes in. Believing is therefore a mere expression of the state, attitude or condition of the heart towards God while faith involves vocalising your believing. For example so many people believe that Jesus came into this world, died on the cross and rose after three days from the dead and ascended to heaven and they end there. That is not faith but believing. Believing alone does not get one to be born again. But faith is believing in all that and then taking a step to confess that Jesus is Lord and receiving him into your heart as the Lord and personal saviour and then start fellowshipping intimately with the Holy Spirit. That is faith in its totality. Put differently, it is possible for someone to believe that

Jesus died and was raised from the dead for his justification and still end up in hell. This is because to merely believe that He died and was raised back to life isn't enough to guarantee salvation. Even demons believe and tremble (James 2:19) but that doesn't mean that they are saved. There is more required for salvation than just believing. You must confess the Lordship of Jesus Christ over your life to be saved.

It is disheartening to note that some people want to relegate or reduce Christianity to some form of belief system. Believing is not good enough. Christianity is not about believing but a constant expression and walk of faith with God. That is why Paul emphasised in James 2:19 *that you believe that there is one God. You do well. Even the demons believe—and tremble.* So it is not enough just to believe. You must go beyond mere believing into the realm of genuine unfeigned faith. Beliefs are thoughts but faith is action. For example when Jesus told Jairos in Mark 9:24 to believe, the man answered and said, *"I believe, please help my unbelief"*. What this man meant is that he believes in Jesus but he does not have faith in healing hence he appeals to the Lord to help him strengthen and develop his faith. The phrase *help my unbelief* depicts or portrays a lack of faith although the man believed in Jesus as a sovereign Messiah. He believed in Jesus as the Messiah but did not have faith that Jesus could bring about a healing. This is contrary to the act of a centurion in Mathew 8:8 who perfectly exercised his faith by saying to Jesus, *"Master I'm not worthy to have you come under my roof but just speak a word and my servant shall be healed"* and it was granted. The bible further records in Luke 8:43-48, an incident whereby many people were pushing and pressing against Jesus as He went because they believed in Him for healing but none is recorded to have been healed except the woman with an issue of blood who took a practical step to exercise her faith for healing by touching the hem of Jesus's garment and instantly she received her healing. Jesus confirmed by proclaiming that her faith had made her well. In other words unlike others who were pressing and pushing Jesus, she put her faith into action hence received her positive results.

In Mark 10:51, Jesus met a certain blind man who cried out to Jesus and said, "*Master, please help me*". In other words he believed in Jesus, he believed that Jesus would heal him. But when Jesus had come He asked him a question, "*What do you want me to do for you?* A religious person might ask, is that not obvious what the man wanted? How come Jesus asks the man what he wants him to do when He is seeing that the man is blind? But Jesus understood how God's system works. He needed the man to have faith to receive his healing. Many people inadvertently think that all they need is to believe, yet believing alone is not enough. It is not about God but about you, because if it was about God, everyone would be healed anywhere, anytime but it is not the case because God demands that we reach unto Him by faith. That is why the Bible says in Luke 4:27 that there were so many sick folks in Jerusalem but not all of them where healed. Why? This was not because of not believing but it was due to lack of faith. They believed in Jesus as the Messiah, the Healer but could not rightly position themselves to receive their healing from Jesus. Only those who took a practical steps of faith and rightly positioned themselves at the right place, at the right time were healed. For example, the lame man by the pool side, ten lepers who took an action to go show themselves to the priest, the crippled man at beautiful gate and Bathemeous who shouted when he heard Jesus passing by, were healed.

Faith That Raises Raise The Dead

It is worth noting that it doesn't take hyper faith for one to be catapulted into the realm of resurrection. Instead, it takes a childlike faith to raise the dead. A child like faith is the one that takes God at His word, and believe God for everything that He says without any wavering, doubt or reasoning. Faith is such a crucial ingredient in matters of raising the dead because it is through faith that we are able to connect with the spirit realm and harness its divine energy to produce results in the natural. Faith is the antenna whose frequency is being tuned to the spiritual waves that come directly from the throne room of heaven. It establishes a direct divine connection with heaven such that when you step on the death scene to command the dead to arise, heaven releases a corresponding divine energy to set that which you have decreed in motion. Faith is the ever empowering awareness of the invisible world and its realities. Therefore, having faith means giving credence to unseen realities. Faith is the ascent out of the time dimension into the eternal realm and since faith acts like an invisible hand that travels across both realms of existence, it is through faith that we are able to re-collect or reinstate a spirit that would have departed from the body, to move from the spirit world and be cast back into its body in the natural realm. When Lazarus died, Jesus said to his disciples, *"Only Believe"*. He strongly said to Martha,

"Didn't I tell you that if you believe, you shall see the glory of God?"

This implies that the glory of God manifested in the raising of the dead is not for everybody but only for those who believe. Moreover, this passage shows Jesus's dialogue with Martha trying to draw out her confession of faith in Him. Jesus was looking for the *now faith* not *future faith.* She believed that Jesus was the resurrection in the future. But Jesus was trying to draw the *now faith* out of her. She had faith to have Jesus healed Lazarus but now that he was dead for four days, she did not have the *resurrection now faith*, that is why Jesus was moved with indignation and deeply troubled to the extent of weeping at the account of their lack of faith. Through her response: "*I know that he will rise again in the resurrection at the last day*", she made reference to the time that had her reality sometime in the future. Although Judgment Day is a set day in the future, she had failed to realize that Jesus had come out of that day and came back to her day, saying in effect, "*Martha, you don't have to wait till that day.*" She didn't realize that the resurrection was not an event, it was a person. Jesus said, "*I am the resurrection.*" Don't be constrained by your lack of understanding of time. Seize your portion right now! He was saying, "*If you believe, you don't have to wait until that day!*" He meant that faith could take you beyond time into the future to bring your future into the present.

There are a myriad of scriptural references that we can apply in the case of resurrection to practically demonstrate how important faith is in raising the dead. Application of scripture in this particular subject helps reinforce a significant understanding of the phenomenon of resurrection. Concerning matters of faith, Jesus strongly contended in Mathew 21:21-22 saying,

> *"Verily, I say unto you, if you shall say to this mountain, Be thou removed, and be thou cast into the sea, and you do not doubt in your heart but believe that those things which you speak shall come to pass, you shall have whatever you say".*

Note that the term, *"mountain"* speak of a situation of impossibility, like facing a dead body and the phrase, *"whatever you ask"* also incorporates the grace to raise the dead or the granting of a request concerning the re-instatement of a spirit that would have been relinquished from the body. Therefore, when applied in the sense of a resurrection, this scripture could read as:

> *"Verily, I say unto you, if you shall say to this spirit of the dead, be thou removed from the spirit world, and be cast back into the body, and do not doubt in your heart but believe that those things which you speak shall come to pass, then you shall raise the dead".*

The Lord Jesus in the verse above gave us the recipe for effecting a change in any situation. In other words, to change any seemingly hopeless situation, what you need do is to declare faith-filled words; talk to the mountain. Sadly, some folks, instead of talking to the mountain choose rather to talk about the mountain and that's not going to change things. As long as you're discussing your challenging situations rather than eyeballing them and commanding a change, you're not going to get the result the Lord Jesus spoke about; the mountain won't move. If your mountain is facing the dead body, it's time to stop talking about it and talk to it! It's time so say *"You, spirit of death, loosen your grip on this man now, in Jesus' Name"* and then begin to rejoice for the answer. This is because faith doesn't speak and watch to see the mountain go; Instead, faith considers the mountain gone once it has spoken! In a related scripture in John 14:12-14 12 Jesus unveiled the divine road map for greatness saying,

"Verily, verily, I say unto you, He that believes in Me, the works that I do, shall he do also; and greater works than these shall he do; because I go to my Father".

Note that, *"greater works"* implies the greatness of what believers can do with the resurrection power of God, as a result of the indwelling presence of the Holy Spirit. Therefore, applied in the sense of resurrection, this could read as :

"Verily, verily, I say unto you, He that believes in Me, the dead whom I have raised, you shall raise them also; and greater multitudes than these shall you raise from the dead, because I go to my Father".

This is to show you the inviolable role faith plays in raising the dead. The above infers that although Jesus was limited in His scope of influence to a smaller geographical setting, the impact of what He accomplished will be multiplied millions of times over as believers in this end time season, step up to their level of greatness by commanding the dead everywhere to arise. Moreover, the above scripture continues in the next verse where Jesus said,

"Whatsoever you shall ask in My name, that will I do, that the Father may be glorified in the Son. If you shall ask any thing in My name, I will do it".

Note that the term, "*Whatsoever*" could also incorporate the raising of the dead because Jesus did not specify exactly what we can ask. It could incorporate our requests directed to God to have the departed spirit returned to its body upon death. Applied in the context of a resurrection, this scripture could therefore be translated and read as:

"And whatsoever departed spirit you shall ask to return to its body, in My name, that will I grant, that the Father may be glorified in the Son. If you ask for the spirit that has departed from the body to come back, in My name, I will do it".

The above thrilling illustrations are meant to show you how crucial faith is as a divine ingredient in birthing forth a resurrection. Smith Wigglesworth, who has been labelled as the Great Apostle of Faith for his acts of resurrection of twenty two people from the dead, tapped into the realm of faith and led to a break out of a global resurrection revival in his generation. How did he do it? *Through faith.* It is such greater dimensions of faith that saw him raise all these people from the dead. Faith is the currency of heaven. It is a medium of exchange for all divine transactions that takes place between heaven and earth or between the realm of eternity and the realm of time. God provided a medium of exchange, valid in Heaven and on earth when He gave us faith. That is why faith is described as the currency or gold standard of the eternal realm. This implies that in the same way we use money to buy things in the natural realm, we use our faith to buy back the departed spirit from the spirit world into the human body. Understand that when someone dies or relinquishes his last breath, there is a spiritual transaction that has taken place between the natural word and the spirit world. Therefore, to bring that departed spirit back into the body, you need to release something in order to receive the departed spirit back. Hence, we pay using our faith. Faith is our purchasing power in the realm of the spirit. If you don't have faith, you are in a *spiritual recession* where resurrection power is concerned, hence you will not be able to command the dead to arise. The Bible makes it crystal clear that *without faith, it is impossible to please God* (Hebrews 11:6). By the same token, *without faith it is impossible to raise the dead.* This is because raising the dead requires that one moves into the spirit realm to command the spirit of the dead to return to its body and travelling into the realm of the spirit requires faith. So, it means if you don't have faith then you won't be able to move into the spirit dimension to command the spirit of the dead to come back because faith is like a hand that travels to extract the departed spirit from the realm of the supernatural and brings it back into the physical body in the natural realm. That is why by reason of faith, *it is easy to raise a dead person than to heal a religious Christian of a headache.* A dead person does not need to have faith to be raised or cooperate with the minister when raising him from the dead. His faith does not work in this instance but that of the minister coupled with the dynamics of the workings of the Holy Ghost. But for a religious person who has a lot of doubt and unbelief, cooperation is needed for him to successfully appropriate his healing, by faith.

Note that the biblically correct way of exercising your faith for a resurrection is not to pray and then look around for see if the dead will arise or not. Instead, you have to ask for the departed spirit to come back and then "*lamba-*

no" it. Jesus admonished us in this regard: *Verily, verily, I say unto you, Whatsoever you shall ask the Father in my name, he will give it you. Until now, you have asked nothing in my name: ask, and you shall receive, that your joy may be full* (John 16:23-24). The word receive in the context of Jesus' teaching above is the Greek *"lambano"*; and it means to take a hold of something and make it yours! Some people ask and keep asking repeatedly for the same thing; that's wrong! You're to ask and then *"lambano"*; that means "*Ask, and take possession*!" Jesus carefully chose His words; He didn't just say "*ask!*" He said, "*Ask, and receive.*" So once you've asked, take a hold of the answer with your spirit and declare, "I've got it; it's mine!" "*Lambano*" connotes some aggressive faith-response from your spirit; that means you don't wait passively for what you've asked to be delivered to you; instead, you go for it! You reach out with your faith and take possession. In other words, you don't pray for the dead and then at the same time be checking if they are any changes on the body. Instead, command the dead to arise and then declare that the death victim is alive and begin to thank God for restoration of life. By declaring that he is alive, you are actually exerting a supernatural influence for heaven to legally endorse the resurrection, thereby compelling all forces of divinity to release the spirit back into the body. Faith is a revelation, *for by faith we are saved through faith and that's not of yourself* (Ephesians 2:8), meaning it's not from the realm of senses but a product of spiritual mechanics. For a deeper revelation and practical guidelines on how to exercise your faith, I would like to kindly refer you to one of my anointed books titled, "*New Revelations Of Faith*" *by Apostle Frequency Revelator.*

The Law of faith

It must be understood that practical demonstration or experimentation is such a vital principle when it comes to the ministry of raising the dead. In other words, it is virtually impossible for the dead to be raised without one taking actions of faith to command the dead to rise up. Death is not automatic. It is either initiated, provoked or set in motion. If there is no corresponding action to validate its manifestation, the dead will not rise up by themselves. If there is no corresponding action of faith that validates, authorises or gives spiritual subjects permission to legally endorse a resurrection, then the dead are not raised. It's as simple as that. You can cry, twirl and twain until your face turns blue but unless you command the dead to arise, they might not be raised. This is because in the realm of the spirit, nothing can be registered as legitimate and acceptable to God if there is no corresponding action effected thereto. Faith without action is as dead as death itself. That is why the Bible concurs in Hebrews 11:6 that *without faith it is impossible to please*

God. By the same token, without corresponding action, demonstration or experimentation, it is impossible for the dead to be raised. The only way you can get to know if you have the *resurrection power* is when you demonstrate your actions of faith by praying for the dead.

How will you raise the dead if you never pray for anyone dead to be raised? The dead are not going to vacate the mortuaries and come into your living room. Instead, you need to be bold enough to go to wherever they are.

The greater truth is that it takes courage and boldness coupled with actions of faith to confront the dead or speak life into a death situation in order to obtain positive results. Jesus is a quintessential example of someone who made practical demonstrations of faith by either touching the casket or speaking directly to the dead to come back to life. According to the law of manifestation, in the realm of the spirit, spiritual subjects are bound to move only when commanded. This is because an action of faith is registered as an input or tangible reality in the realm of the spirit that gives substantial material or license for spiritual subjects to produce whatever results you need. That is why Jesus said *whatever you bind on earth shall be bound in heaven and whatever you release on earth shall be loosed in heaven.* This implies that you need to act on your faith by binding and loosing so that heaven will respond to your actions of faith by releasing a corresponding divine energy to set that which you declare in motion in order to produce the results of what the word talks about. If you don't demonstrate your actions of faith, where do you expect God to get the material needed to magnetise the departed spirit and bring it back into its body? This is because actions of faith are a critical mass and heavy weight substance in the spirit realm that is needed to cause the dead to come back to life. That is why the resurrection power of God will not be precipitated down to earth if there are no corresponding actions of faith to validate or authenticate its release.

But what exactly constitutes the actions of faith? Actions can be expressed in two different ways; it's either they come in the form of *words* or *demonstrations.* Do you know that everything that is created, whether living or dead has sound waves, a rhythm embedded in it and a voice that hears and obeys when commanded to. By the same token, even a dead corpse has a sound waves and a rhythm that responds when you command it to come back to life. It might not have an active mouth to express itself anymore but it has a rhythm that hears. Do you remember that Jesus spoke to a fig tree such that it listened and obeyed the results of which it instantly withered? If a fig tree, an inanimate object, worse than a dead corpse could hear the voice of Jesus, obey and wither instantly, how much more would we not speak to the dead body and command it to come back to life. Even though it might not be showing any signs of movement in the natural realm, in the realm of the spirit, it surely has a rhythm that responds when commanded to. Armed with this revelation, it makes you realise that your mission to raise the dead is as easy as taking a stroll through a park.

CHAPTER TWO

SECOND DIMENSION:

THE DIMENSION OF THE ANOINTING

Despite its heightened degree of popularity as a divine phenomenon, the anointing can be one of those subjective biblical phrases that can mean different things to different people based on their understanding and interpretation. When someone says, "*That man is anointed*" *or* "*She is an anointed singer,*" or "*That was an anointed worship set,*" what exactly are they saying? Do they really understand what exactly they are implying? Has it assimilated into the depths of their being what the anointing is all about? This is because not every Christian seem to have caught a clear understanding and revelation of what '*the anointing*' is. It appears that the *anointing* is understood or perceived by different denominations differently, especially in these modern days, whereby almost everything is said to be *anointed.* It is against this background that accurately and comprehensively defining the *anointing* has become a subject of great interest to the writer since an attempt has been made in this publication to produce a substantial body of revelations and practical scenarios devoted to understanding the *anointing.*

It is of paramount significance to unveil the divine truth that while an attempt has been made by various scholars and theologians across a broad spectrum of both Christian classical and charismatic cycles to try and explain *the anointing,* it has been unanimously observed that many definitions and explanations encapsulated in the description of the anointing suffer limitations of being a one sided, theoretical view which lacks both practical and revelation perspectives. The greater truth is that defining the *anointing* from only a theological perspective does not bring about an in-depth understanding of the concept because it is not enough *to just talk about a concept.* Instead, it matters most when *one demonstrates it.* Metaphorically speaking, in the same way just one drop of water is not sufficient to cool up the whole engine, a one sided perspective to the description of *the anointing* is not enough to trigger a profound or in-depth understanding of such a broad divine phenomenon. It is therefore highly imperative in our attempt to dissect the subject of the *anointing* that we define it from a comprehensive and holistic perspective by examining it from all angles *(through incorporating both theological, practical and revelational perspectives).* In this regard, *three* critical definitions seem to suffice in the description of the term *anointing:*

Firstly, the anointing is an *impartation* of God's supernatural ability upon an available and yielded vessel to enable it to do His work efficiently and effectively. In other words, it is a divine ability infused upon a vessel to enable it to operate like God on earth. To operate like God means to assume the faculties of God such that you are able to talk as God talks, see as God sees, think as God thinks and act as God acts. Therefore, the anointing is the empowerment for us to live the way Christ desires us to live through demonstrating the Kingdom of Heaven on earth. To be anointed means to be empowered by God to do a particular task, hence metaphorically speaking, the anointing could therefore be best described as *God on flesh doing those things that flesh cannot do.* In other words, it is God doing those things only He can do, and doing them through a flesh and blood, earthly vessel (2 Corinthians 4:7).

Secondly, the anointing is a divine *enablement* of the Holy Ghost geared to equip and empower either an individual or a group of people for service and accomplishment of divine tasks or assignments. In other words, it is the Supernatural enablement manifested by the presence of the Holy Spirit operating upon or through an individual or corporate group of people to produce the works of Jesus. In a literal sense, it is the presence of the Holy Spirit being smeared upon someone. It is literally the smearing of the substance of the anointing of the Holy Spirit into our lives that makes us able to do what He wants done *excellently and exceptionally*. It is when the Holy Spirit supernaturally enables you to do something that you cannot take credit for by natural talent or physical means. In other words, it is the grace given by the Holy Spirit that makes an individual a "*superman*" by performing beyond the level of human talent, reasoning, skill, ability and intelligence.

Thirdly, the anointing is an *endowment* of a spiritual substance upon both a living and non-living object to enable it to perform beyond human or natural limitations. In this context, to be anointed by God means to be supernaturally endowed with divine assistance to do the appointed task for which God has called you. Therefore, the anointing is that divine energy that comes upon you and separates you from yourself and fills you with His power such that when you speak, it is like God speaking and when you act, it is like God acting. In other words, it is the overflowing life of Jesus which endows supernatural strength, enabling a person to perform a special task or function in an office he is called and appointed to. Therefore to be anointed by God is not only to be hand-picked, but also to be endowed or empowered by Him for the task or position to which He has called you.

The Essence of The Anointing

In an endeavour to establish an in-depth, profound and significant level of understanding of this divine phenomenon it is of paramount importance that three aspects which form the core of the definition of the *anointing* be clarified. The critical or central terminology used in the description of the anointing which requires further clarification is ***impartation, enablement and endowment.*** This is meant to facilitate a solid understanding of certain expressions and terminology that is used in the description of this divine phenomenon of the *anointing*. It is therefore not my solemn intent to create a doctrine around this concept but to provide revelation guidelines which you could use in a view to explore this divine phenomenon.

First definition:

****The anointing is an impartation of God's supernatural ability upon a vessel to enable it to do His work efficiently and effectively.***

The use of the term " *impartation*" in the description of the anointing implies that it is the Holy Ghost who rubs Himself intimately on a vessel during the process or act of transferring the anointing. In this context, the word "ANOINT" describes the procedure or practice of rubbing or smearing a person or thing, usually with perfumed oil for the purpose of healing, setting apart, or embalming. The original Hebrew word for *'anointing'* is *'mischah'* which means *'smearing'*. In this sense, the word anoint in the Hebrew language speaks about a rubbing in and an impartation of oil hence, the anointing can strictly be spoken of as an impartation. By the same token, the original Greek word for *'anointing'* is *'chrisma'* which means *'a rubbing in'*. In other words, there is a *'rubbing in'*, a tangible impartation of the substance of the anointing upon a person when he is anointed. In view of the above, the term *impartation* therefore implies that a spiritual transaction has taken place in the supernatural. In other words, something tangible, visible and feel-able has actually been transacted in the spirit. In other words, something tangible has been given, transacted or exchanged in the supernatural or realm of the spirit. There is an undeniable evidence of a tangible impartation of a divine substance that has taken place. Therefore, in the same way a man jumps into a pool of water and comes out drenched from the crown of his head to the souls of his feet, it is impossible for one to say that he has received an anointing and not show it because the anointing is a tangible spiritual substance hence, the evidence will speak for itself.

The optimum usage of twin concepts of "*efficiency and effectiveness*" in the description of the term *anointing* implies that with the anointing, not only are tasks executed with divine speed and acceleration but with a significant degree of *accuracy, precision and excellence.* This means that with the anointing, what could have taken years to achieve is accomplished in a twinkling of an eye and what could have taken ages to figure out is achieved in a season, what could have taken kilojoules of energy to complete is accomplished with less effort and metaphorically speaking, what could have taken months to conceive is given birth to in a flip of a divine moment. In other words greater, abundant and humongous work is done quicker, easier and better within a short period of time. This is the *essence of the anointing.* Expressed differently, the anointing could therefore be described as an *impartation* of God's spirit of Love, Wisdom, Power, Riches and Creativity upon men and women all over the world to empower and enable them to complete the task of reaching the world with the gospel in a view to usher an unprecedented avalanche of billions of souls across the globe into the kingdom of God. Therefore, the anointing is nothing but the very traits of God which He has made available to all mankind so that we can operate more effectively to fulfil the great commission of God. In other words, it is the supernatural dimension of man which reflects God's very nature and characteristics embedded upon humanity.

Second definition:

**** The anointing is a divine enablement of the Holy Ghost designed or geared to equip and empower either an individual or a group of people for service or accomplishment of divine tasks or assignments.***

The term "*enablement*" in the description of the anointing implies that anything *(both living and non-living)* that comes into contact with the Holy Ghost can receive God ability. In other words, it acquires the properties of the spirit realm and grace to perform or function with the faculties of God, thereby operating with heavenly efficiency. In essence, the anointing can be spoken of as a grace given to a vessel by the Holy Ghost to enable him to accomplish certain divine tasks in a generation. It must therefore be fully understood in this regard that it is the Holy Ghost who administers (*measures, allocates, disseminate)* the anointing upon a vessel. The Holy Ghost is the originator or source of the anointing, hence without the Holy Ghost, there is *no such thing as the anointing* because the anointing is God's lubricated presence that comes by the Holy Spirit. For example, the anointing on Jesus's life came by the Holy Spirit (Luke 4:18; Acts 10:38). It actually took the Holy Spirit to descend upon Him like dove so that He would receive the *anointing.* As a matter of fact, Jesus is called *Christ* because of the *anointing.* It is the anointing that made Him who He was. In other words He was defined by the measure of the *anointing* upon His life. This is to tell you how critical the manifested presence of the Holy Spirit is to tapping into greater depths of the anointing.

It is therefore highly imperative in this regard that a divine correction or perspective of the anointing be ushered to demystify the myths and religious perceptions and misconceptions created around the subject of the *anointing.* There is a common Christian cliché spoken across a broad spectrum of the Christian faith that God does not look for our *ability,* but *availability* and consequentially many people tend to avail themselves to God and try very hard to do God's work without His ability. On that note, it must therefore be fully comprehended that not only does God wants our availability but He wants us to receive His ability too. Metaphorically speaking, when God gives you the anointing, He receives the glory in return because the anointing is what manifests His glory hence the anointing belongs to man and the glory belong to God. The anointing is correspondingly to man what the glory is to God. That is why the Bible says *let the weak say I'm strong* (Joel 3:10). Why? Because in that realm of confession, you are no longer operating using your own ability but God's ability. Therefore, to avail yourself is one side of the story. The other side is to learn to receive His ability (*which is the anointing*) from Him. This is the essence of *the anointing*.

To give you a historical perspective and insight into the phenomenon of the *anointing*, when God created man in the Garden of Eden in His own *image* and *likeness*, God gave man His own characteristics, traits and abilities. In the context of the above revelation, the word " *image*" infers that we look exactly like God while the word "*likeness*" implies that we function exactly like him. In other words, by virtue of being created in the *likeness* of God, man was *enabled* by God to move in both the realm of the spirit to commune with God and also function in the realm of the natural and interact with animals. This means that when we are anointed, we have the same characteristics and abilities as that of God. Therefore, the anointing in simple terms can be referred to as an enablement from God to man while at the same time, man also inherits the qualities or the ability to impart the anointing that he has to others in his sphere of contact. In other words, the anointing represents the characteristics, traits and abilities of God Himself. It is for this reason that the anointing is such a delicate and precious heavenly commodity hence we should be interested in getting more of God's anointing to become more like him by being transformed into His image and likeness. The good news is that God's anointing is available to every one of us and those who diligently seek it and are willing to use it for the extension of God's kingdom are the frst candidates to be considered as recipients of this amazing divine treasure.

The phrase "*divine assignment*" specified in the definition of the anointing above implies such tasks as pre-destined callings, offices and divine assignments which God ordained before the foundations of the world such as the work of ministry, manifested in preaching the gospel of the Lord Jesus Christ, salvation of souls, displaying the resurrection power of God through miracles, signs and wonders, ministering to Lord in prayer, healing the sick, deliverance, raising the dead, church planting and establishment, operating the fivefold ministry graces and gifts of the spirit as well as other administrative functions of the Kingdom. Contrary to what a multitude of people presume, not everybody is anointed to be a preacher, although preaching is central to the precipitation of the gospel. Instead, others are anointed as Kingdom Millionaires to finance the gospel while others have the anointing for church administration. However, the nature of the assignment varies depending on the level of calling, degree of the anointing manifested and so forth. It must also be expressly understood that not all believers have the same callings and the same measure of the anointing although God deals with all of us justly. Instead, believers have been entrusted with tasks, visions and assignments of various scales for example some are responsible for local, regional, national and global visions, hence the measure of the anointing which an individual can manifest is directly proportional or tantamount to the size of his God-given vision. It is therefore evident that every individual has been called to accomplish a specific divine task in the kingdom and with it comes a specific measure of the anointing.

Third definition:

**** The anointing is an endowment of a spiritual substance upon either a living and non-living object or vessel to enable it to perform beyond human or natural limitations.***

The term "*endowment*" in the description of the anointing implies a complete synthesis, blending, fusion or infilling of a measureless substance of the anointing, brought through the tidal waves of the spirit, running down or flooding one's spirit as in the case of the anointing poured on Aaron and running down his beard (Psalms 133:1). It describes the way and nature by which the anointing is imparted. It gives us an exact and accurate portrait or picture of how the anointing is poured right from the crown of our heads to the soles of our feet and how the entirety of our being is drenched into the anointing during impartation. Therefore, in its original usage in this context, the word *anoint* means to pour oil upon someone or something as a means of conveying a supernatural blessing and endowment for a task.

The accompanying phrase "*spiritual substance*" in the description of the anointing implies that the anointing is a tangible commodity or a real heavenly product that is transferred or transacted from the realm of the spirit to the natural realm to enable man to operate with heavenly efficiency on earth. Therefore, it is a spiritual substance in the sense of its tangibility, feel-ability and visibility when manifested in the natural realm. Moreover, the corresponding term "*vessel or object*"implies that the anointing can be imparted upon anything whether living *(In the case of human beings)* or non-living *(in the case of clothes and handkerchiefs)*.It must be expressly understood that the anointing does not only stay on human vessels but upon ministration, it can linger in the air or atmosphere, upon buildings, in the water, on the ground and on any object in the natural realm. The practical demonstration of the anointing through the shadow of Peter in the early church and the ministration though handkerchiefs taken from Paul's body as well as the bones of Elisha which still retained the anointing to the extent of raising someone from the dead who came into contact with Elisha's bones more than four hundred years after he had died is an ample evidence of this reality (2 Kings 13:21). The good news is that Jesus has provided the same presence of the Holy Spirit for us in our earthly ministries that He had in His earthly ministry!

THE PURPOSE FOR THE ANOINTING

There are SEVEN principal reasons given to me by revelation as to why the anointing is given or released from heaven. Firstly, it must be understood that in the realm of God's power, the anointing is strictly for *SERVICE and* not for personal use, fame, show-off or celebrity purposes. In the natural realm, every product or substance is originally designed to satisfy a specific need, for example, a car was created for transportation purposes and a house for residential purposes. By the same token, the anointing was created as a spiritual substance or divine commodity to enable man to accomplish specific assignments or divine tasks in the kingdom. This is the *essence of the anointing.* The anointing that is upon you is for service since God anoints you with His Spirit to empower you to do the work He has called you to do. Therefore the anointing is not given for the vessel it flows through but it is given for the one it flows to.

The level of anointing you have determines your level of productivity. This implies that you don't need the anointing if you are not doing anything because you get anointed for a mission. It is because of the anointing that you can be like God in the demonstration of power. Note that it is a calling or assignment that comes first then after that the release of the anointing. Contrary to what some folks think, God does not give someone an anointing first and then later on calls that person for ministry. Instead, God originates with a divine call or assignment, and after that gives man His ability *(the anointing)* to fulfil the assignment He has called him to accomplish. Therefore, one of the easiest ways of knowing whether someone is called or not is through gauging the level of anointing up his life. In actual fact, the evidence of a calling is the anointing upon a vessel. This is a *benchmark of the anointing.*

The greater truth is that there is an intricate connection between the *calling* and the *anointing.* When you find your purpose or calling, you have found the anointing. Until you know who you are and what your purpose on earth is, you will not be able to find your anointing because the anointing is given for you to carry out your assignment. Metaphorically speaking, the anointing is like a hidden treasure that is wrapped up in the assignment hence, if you want to unveil it, you need to reap open first the assignment and then you will be able to get it. Strictly speaking, the anointing is given to those who are *"called"* by God to do His will. For example, when God calls someone into a particular office, He anoints them with supernatural power and ability to carry out the functions of that office. When we understand this principle, it becomes easy to recognize those who are called and anointed by God for the office they stand in because they seem to have a supernatural endowment to carry out the functions of that office with ease and excellence. It also becomes easy to recognize when someone is *not* called and anointed to an office because they are *not* able to perform the duties of that office in a manner consistent with the excellence required by the Lord for that office. Against this background, it is therefore important to precautiously admonish that no one should ever attempt to stand in a ministry office without the call of God and the anointing that comes with the office. Not only is it dangerous for the individual personally to attempt to stand in ministry offices if they have not been called and anointed to that office, but it can also bring great harm to the body of Christ just like what happened to *Aaron and Miriam when they tried to stand in an office that they were not called to by God* (Numbers 12:1-10).

Moreover, the anointing is also given for a *fifth fold* purpose initially unveiled by the Prophet Isaiah in the Old Testament dispensation and latter echoed or reiterated by the Lord Jesus Christ in the New Testament dispensation. The prophet Isaiah, looking forward in time by the Spirit of God, saw the One through whom the yoke of Satan's oppression shall be destroyed *because of the anointing* (Isaiah 10:27). To substantiate this revelation with reference to scriptural evidence, Jesus clearly illustrated the purpose of God's anointing upon His life when He made a public declaration or pronunciation of its availability (Luke 4:10-19). In this context, Jesus quoted the scripture of (Isaiah 61: 1), where He boldly declared that,

The spirit of the Lord God is upon Me, because the Lord has anointed Me to preach good tidings to the poor; He has sent Me to heal the broken hearted, to proclaim liberty to the captives, and opening of the prison to those who are bound; to proclaim the acceptable year of the Lord.

On the basis of the above mentioned scripture, it is therefore evident that the *fifth fold* purpose of the anointing is *to propagate the world with the gospel of the Lord Jesus, to heal the sick, to destroy the works of darkness and liberate humanity from all entanglement of the web of evil, to command breakthrough and open supernatural doors for humanity and to make prophetic declarations in specific seasons.*

In addition, the purpose of the anointing is also revealed in Isaiah 10:27 where Isaiah declared *that it shall come to pass that on that day the burden shall be uplifted and the yoke destroyed BY REASON OF THE ANOINTING*. This implies that besides the *fifth fold* purpose unveiled by Jesus Christ in Luke 4:10-19, the anointing is also given *to break the yoke and chains of evil, so as to activate man towards the fulfilment of their destiny in God and to equip and empower them with power to move in the supernatural.*

In view of the above, the fact that Jesus made a public proclamation in Luke4:18that *the Spirit of the Lord is upon Him*, tells us that He knew and was conscious of the fact that the anointing was upon Him because you cannot announce what you do not have. In actual fact, He was announcing the purpose or reason for which He has received the *anointing*. He was proclaiming it to the people using scriptures from the prophet Isaiah that the *anointing* was upon His life for the people. It was therefore left for the people themselves to place a demand on the anointing by faith and make a withdrawal of that anointing into their lives. It is therefore undeniably evident that the anointing is primarily given to preach the gospel, heal the sick, cast out devils, and fulfil God's will on earth. This implies that the anointing is the reason behind the manifestation of miracles, signs and wonders. In the absence of the anointing, the sick are not healed, the captives are not set free, the demonic possessed are not delivered and the dead are not . This is the *essence of the anointing* .

Jesus is our practical model and example of how we should operate in the realm of *the anointing*. Without reference to Jesus, the revelation of the phenomenon of the *anointing* will not be understood in depth. In a practical sense, Jesus walked constantly in the *anointing* to the extent that He began His ministry with a *public declaration of the Anointing* (Luke 4:18-19). This is to show you that even Jesus was so grossly dependent on the anointing to do the mighty works He did. That is why Luke records that "*on a certain day, as He was teaching, the power of the Lord was present to heal them*" (Luke 5:17). In the context of this scripture, the phrase "*power of the Lord*" speaks of *the anointing.* That means that even Jesus himself needed the anointing just like any one of us, to fulfil God's mission on earth. Ideally speaking, when we speak about the greater dimensions of the anointing in which Jesus tapped into during His earthly ministry, some people are tempted to think that, it is because He was the Son of God that He was able to launch into the greater depths of the miraculous. And, of course, He was but what they fail to realize is that *He as the Son of God was one thing* and *He as a person ministering was another thing.* Jesus did not minister as the Son of God but He ministered as a mere man anointed by the Holy Spirit. If Jesus had been ministering as the Son of God, He wouldn't have needed to be anointed. Or, if He had been ministering as God manifested in the flesh, would God have needed to be anointed? Therefore, Jesus also had to be anointed before He could start moving in God's power because He had laid aside His mighty power and glory as the Son of God when He became a man. Although in person He was the Son of God, in power He was not the Son of God.

To cement this revelation with reference to further scriptural and theological evidence, it is of paramount significance to unveil the divine revelation of the word " *Christ*". The word *Christ* is a Greek word. Why the English translators failed to translate it in the Bible, I don't know but that failure has cost us a great revelation. The word *Christ* isn't Jesus' last name. It is not a title but a word with a very significant meaning. It is a reference to *the Anointed* and *the Anointing* that was on Him and in Him. Christ actually means *anointed.* To anoint is literally "*to pour on, smear all over, or rub into.*" So the anointing of God is to have God poured on, smeared all over, and rubbed onto you. The Anointing of God is God on flesh doing only those things God can do. In the same way, the word "*Christians*" means more than just followers of Jesus. It means "*the anointeds*". This implies that the same yoke-destroying anointing that was on Jesus is available to you. This is because you can't separate the *Anointed* and the *anointing.* If you're in the *Anointed One,* then you're in *the anointing.* This implies that if you're "*in Christ,*" there's an anointing for everything you're called to do, no matter how small or how great the task is. That's what the Apostle Paul meant when he said,

I can do all things through Christ (the Anointed and His Anointing) which strengthens me"(Philippians 4:13).

Notice that he didn't say "*who strengthens me"* but "*which strengthens me."* He was not talking about *Christ (the person)* but he was talking about *Christ (the anointing).* Sixthly, the anointing is given to bring the glory of God into manifestation. This is its ultimate purpose in the kingdom. In essence, you get to see the glory of God through the *anointing.* In other words, the anointing is what connects you to the glory of God. God's presence and power are resident in the *anointing,* hence any man of God who taps into the realm of the anointing and manifests miracles, signs and wonders ushers the glory of God on the scene. In essence, the anointing reveals or manifests the glory of God because where the anointing flows, Christ is glorified. In Acts 10:38, the bible speaks of *how God anointed Jesus of Nazareth with the Holy Ghost and with power, who went about doing good, and healing all that were oppressed of the devil, for God was with Him.* This implies that the anointing is what certifies, reinforces, establishes and authenticates God's unwavering supremacy, divine plans, purpose in the light of His creation. In the absence of the anointing, the glory is not revealed. However, some people inadvertently presume that the anointing and the glory is one and the same thing. On the other extreme end, some are just so obsessed about the anointing and in the process they neglect the glory that brings that anointing. That is why in this end time dispensation there is an emphasis in the supernatural for a progressive transition from the realm of the anointing to the realm of God's glory and this is what forms the central theme of the end time message. Metaphorically speaking, the anointing is like the light. The light is what manifests the glory of the sun. Without the sun, there is no light and by the same token without the glory, there is no anointing. But it is the light which makes manifest the glory of the sun. In the same manner, it is the anointing that manifests the glory of God.

Lastly, the anointing is given to bring both the realm of the natural and the realm of the supernatural into harmony or synchronisation to function together or collectively to fulfil God's purpose. In this case, the anointing is like a lubricant that is smeared between two rough surfaces so that there is no friction between them. To illustrate this revelation with reference to scriptural evidence, let me take you back into the Garden of Eden where the original man was created. Adam was created a spirit being and he travelled in both realms of existence without any difficulty. Adam would easily move in the realm of the spirit and talk to God and after that he would move back to the natural and talk to his animals. To him, moving from the realm of the natural to the realm of the spirit was like moving from this bedroom into the living room. Both the realm of the natural and the realm of the spirit were so intricately connected to fulfil God's purpose. But after the fall of man, both realms of existence were torn apart. Anyone who moved from the realm of the natural into the realm of the spirit became a stranger, vice versa. The rhythm, the harmony and flow of energy which connected both these realms was lost and this is the main reason why God says He is going to dissolve the contents of both heaven and earth and then create a new heaven and earth because both realms are no longer in harmony. Therefore, after the fall, man had to struggle to access the supernatural because of the lost connection and moving into the supernatural now requires him to pay a price by undertaking certain spiritual exercises such as fasting and praying and waiting on God, yet in the beginning man would just peep into the spirit without fasting or prayer. Prayer became a means to connect back to God after the fall of man.

The anointing therefore was given to act as a fuel in the realm of the spirit to lubricate the realm of the spirit so that man can easily travel across both realms of God. To illustrate the disharmony between these two realms of existence, in the realm of the spirit, objects like handkerchiefs, jackets and trees, can float, live and even travel without any attention but in the natural they cannot do that. But when the anointing is imparted upon them, such objects can be given God's ability so that they can function exactly like the objects in the spirit. That is why after Paul transmitted the anointing into his handkerchief, it performed miracles because it acquired God's ability which is the same ability that is given to objects in the realm of the spirit. So it is therefore evident that the anointing is what brings both the supernatural and the natural realm to work together in harmony thus fulfilling God's original master plan and purpose about the universe. Now, having caught this revelation, you can no longer play with the anointing because you now know how valuable and expensive it is in fulfilling God's purpose, not only on earth but universally. The anointing is a tangible liquid substance that rains directly from heaven. No wonder why in this last dispensation, it transmutes itself into supernatural oil. This is the essence of the Anointing.

THE ANALOGY OF THE ANOINTING

THE NATURE AND OPERATION OF THE ANOINTING

THE INFLOW AND OUTFLOW OF THE ANOINTING

Operating in the anointing speaks of understanding the greater, deeper and profound depths of how to flow in the manifestation of the anointing and learning to channel it in a specific direction. It also speaks of learning to flow with the nature and character of manifestation, trend, pattern, and fluctuations of the anointing from meeting to meeting, from place to place, from realm to realm and from one dimension to the other. It must be expressly understood that the anointing does not operate in a similar fashion every time. In terms of its operation, there are times when the anointing would generally come upon a congregation in a slow and intermittent fashion depending on the workings of the Holy Ghost. However, there are times when the anointing would just fall upon the whole congregation simultaneously like a cloud of power or heavy rain falling upon the masses. This happened in the upper room (Acts 2:1-4), in the house prayer meeting (Acts 4:31), and in Cornelius' house (Acts 10:44, 45). In such instances, we may call it an *'outpouring'* of the Holy Spirit. Therefore, if you want to understand how the anointing operates, it is of paramount significance that you understand first how the Holy Spirit operates because He is the one who administers the anointing.

There are various substances or natural phenomena which can be used in the *analogy of the anointing* to demonstrate explicitly how the anointing flows in the supernatural. This is because there are certain divine truths that can be best illustrated, explained and understood with reference to physical phenomena. The bible says in Hebrews 11:1 that *the things which are in the natural are a shadow, copy or exact representation of the things which are in the supernatural.*This means that if we have to catch a glimpse of how things are in the supernatural, it is always best that we look into the natural order of things. Hence, in an endeavour to reinforce a significant understanding of spiritual phenomena, it is always wise to illustrate them with reference to physical phenomena which people are acclimatised to. Jesus always used physical things to illustrate spiritual realities, for example when He wanted to illustrate how faith operates, He used the picture of a mountain to portray its operation. In Mathew 21:21, He declared that "*If you say to this mountain be thou removed and be cast into the sea, you shall have whatever you say*" and when He wanted to strengthen their faith in the supernatural, he used a tree as an illustration by cursing its roots and it withered instantly.

In our *analogy of the anointing*, the following substances or natural phenomenon have been used to demonstrate practically how the anointing operates. These are *the flow of electricity, the flow of water as a substance, the flow of air, the flow of rain, the flow of clouds, the flow of a river and the flow of the rays of the sun.* Each of these illustrates a different aspect of how the anointing operates in the supernatural. If only you could grasp an understanding of how this physical phenomenon operates in the natural realm, it will be much easier for you to understand how the anointing operates in the spiritual realm. Therefore, this seventh fold illustration and *analogy of the anointing* is meant to reinforce an in-depth understanding of the *phenomenon of the anointing* so that believers across the body of Christ globally could easily flow and operate in greater depths of the anointing.

From the view of the supernatural, the anointing operates on the basis of the twin processes and principles of "*divine connectivity and conductivity*". Illustrating this concept with reference to how electricity flows in the natural realm to a larger extent reinforces an acute understanding this divine phenomenon since the things in the natural realm are a shadow of these things in the supernatural. It must therefore be expressly understood that in terms of its divine nature, characteristics features and manifestation, the anointing operates just like electricity. Electricity is a good symbol of the anointing of God since there are many observable facts in electricity that are tied up to the way the anointing flows. The concept of natural electricity is therefore a foretaste or a glimpse of the anointing that flows in the realm of the spirit. Just as electricity is in the natural, so is the anointing to the spiritual. Metaphorically, the anointing could therefore be spoken of as God's electricity operating in the supernatural realm.

The anointing is the electricity of heaven!

This is because the anointing is a heavenly materiality, perceptible to the touch and capable to be touched. It is a tangible spiritual substance that can be felt, touched and experienced by multitudes. Just like electricity, the anointing is meticulously governed by spiritual laws and principles in the realm of the supernatural. According to the natural laws of electricity, before electricity could flow, there must be an *inflow* and an *outflow* of electricity. In a like manner, in the realm of the anointing, there is such a thing called an "*inflow*" *and an "outflow" of the anointing.* In the realm of the spirit, the *inflow* of the anointing speaks of the divine outpouring or impartation of the anointing by the Holy Ghost "*flowing into*" the human spirit while the *outflow* is the end–result or manifestations that takes place as the anointing is "*flowing out*" of the human spirit of a yielded vessel to touch the lives of multitudes of people in his sphere of contact. In a ministerial context, God uses our spirits as a channel to transmit the anointing to the congregation *(outflow)* by first pouring His anointing into our spirits *(inflow)*. So, our spirit becomes the vehicle by which the Holy Spirit uses in order to flow and bless mankind. It must be expressly understood in this respect that in a ministerial context, the Holy Spirit does not put aside or bypass you and starts touching the people as what some folks might think. If that was the case, then in every church gathering we would be having enormous records of the move of the Spirit on a daily basis. Instead, the Holy Spirit has to pass systematically as the ark of glory in your spirit man first and He has to flow through your soul and body and then touches the people you are ministering to. Therefore, how great God can truly use you depends to a greater extent on the development of your spirit man, the renewal of your mind and the consecration of your body. Therefore, when you minister in the anointing, you also are a beneficiary of what is flowing through you. In turn, you experience a greater freedom and magnification of the reality of His Presence in your life. Therefore, it is evident that in every manifestation of the anointing, there is always an *inflow* and an *outflow*.

To cement this revelation with reference to a typological example, a battery has latent electricity stored inside it but as long as the *plus* and the *minus* ends of the battery are not connected to each other there is no outflow, regardless of the degree of voltage contacted by the battery. But the moment you put a wire from the *plus* to the *minus* end, then electrons starts flowing through. By the same token, as long as one is not connected in the spirit or rightly positioned in the spirit dimension, the anointing might not flow through him. In a practical sense, if for example seven people are in a queue for healing or any other ministerial purposes and an anointed person touches the first person in the queue, the anointing flows through these vessels and if their spirits are open and their conductivity level is good, the anointing can flow through all of them resulting in them falling under the power. However if somehow their spirits are closed or their conductivity level is poor, then nothing might happen depending of course on the degree of manifestation of the anointing and the level and dimension of anointing the minister is operating at. This is how the anointing flows. In one of his books, John G. Lake describes an experience in his life when the anointing of the Spirit of God came upon him and it was so powerful that when he laid hands on one of the sick person, the person who ushered the sick felt the power of God flow from John G. Lake into the sick person and then out of the sick person into the usherer and he got thrown backwards. This is how the anointing flows. In a related incident, Jesus said to Kenneth Hagin,

> *Tell the people that I told you to tell them that if they will believe that you're anointed—and will receive the anointing, the anointing will flow from your hands into their body and will drive out their sickness or their disease, or will effect a healing or a cure in them."*

This is unequivocally an exact illustration and portrait of how the anointing operates in the supernatural realm. Just like electricity is in the natural, the anointing is explosive in nature and highly inflammable as a divine substance. In the natural realm, if electricity is properly connected, it can bless you and multitudes of other people. However, if it is not properly connected, it can explode and do more harm than good. So, the power of electricity works in both directions. As much as it is strict to operate natural electricity, it is also strict to operate in the anointing. That is why when Eli's sons died because of lighting strange fires, He was not even allowed to mourn or let alone attend the funeral. This is because God demands liability and accountability for every mistake performed in the anointing and the anointing is so sacred, holy and precious that He demands high levels of consecration before He places it on anybody. Hence, philosophically speaking, an anointing is a divine qualification and credential in the spirit realm. That means, you don't accidentally stumble or fall into the anointing but you qualify as a vessel to move or operate in that dimension of the anointing. To substantiate this revelation with further practical evidence, Kenneth Hagin says that,

Electricity is God's power in the natural realm.

Physically, you can take a little electric shock and sometimes a little static electricity. You feel it and shake it off. It doesn't affect your body. But if you grab hold of a lamp that's got a short in it and that power hits you, you jump and holler! You can't stand there all day holding on to that lamp. In fact, even 110 volts will kill you under certain circumstances. And if you move up to higher voltage, it will fry your hide!

Moreover, just like electricity in the natural, the anointing has a conductivity level. The flow of the anointing depends of the conductivity level of the people being ministered to. According to the law of electricity, the amount of electricity that can flow through an object to a larger extent depends on how good or bad the conductor is. Hence in the realm of electricity there are *good conductors of electricity* and also *bad conductors of electivity*. For example, under normal circumstances, wood, water, rubber are bad conductors of electricity while steel, zinc and iron are good conductor of electricity. *By the same token, each person in the spiritual realm has a different conductivity level.* Some people are good conductors of the anointing meaning that the anointing flows easily through them. They react easily to the substance of the anointing. On the other extreme end, some people are poor conductors of the anointing and such people could stand before the power or the anointing of God in a worship service or meeting and they are touched only a little or not touched at all. In other words, they can be spectators in a service where the anointing is flowing mightily, evidenced by people falling under the power, yet they are just looking around and wondering what on earth is going on.

There is no scriptural basis for establishing the spirituality of the individual by whether he falls under the power of the Holy Spirit or not. However, those who fall under the power are more yielded and sensitive to God while those who do not are resistive. Such differences in people's conductivity levels could be highly attributable to people's spiritual receptivity, diversity in background, nature, philosophical affiliation, ideological affiliations, belief systems, reasoning capacities, emotional and mental balances, attitude, expectancy levels and other myriad of external factors or influences. However, while the divine phenomenon of people *falling under the power* has been so much popularly advertised in the current set up in the church, there are other divergent manifestation of *the anointing* which God is increasingly unleashing over the body of Christ as believers are more yielded to new ways and moves of God. While believers have so much been acclimatised to the phenomenon of *people falling under the power*, new manifestations *such as people running under the power, dancing under the power, laughing under the power, jumping under the power, shaking hysterically under the power, flying under the power as well as floating under the power* are increasingly becoming a common experience as God is unleashing the fullness of His *anointing* in these end times.

CHAPTER THREE

THE THIRD DIMENSION:

THE DIMENSION OF THE MANTLE

A mantle is a spiritual covering that comes or rests upon an individual in order to exercise a heightened degree of authority or dominion over a territory. It is an emblem of God's manifest presence in the natural realm.

The greater truth is that mantles fall upon those who move in the realm of territorial dominion and is given to enable individuals to govern, rule, reign, enforce, subdue, conquer, and enthrone territories in the realm of the spirit on behalf of the Kingdom. In its original context, the word, *"mantle"* refers to a cloak, jacket or a sleeveless garment worn over other clothes; a figurative cloak symbolising pre-eminence or authority, glory, kindness, excellence, essence or courage. The mantle is therefore a thick covering of the anointing resting upon a human vessel for a permanent ordination into a specific office. Just before the Lord releases or cast a new *mantle* upon an individual for ordination into a specific office, He will often "*dis-mantle'* that individual's previous level of service. The "*dismantling*" process might not be comfortable but it produces a greater weight of glory as penned by the apostle, Paul. Between the process of "*mantling*" and "*dismantling*", the recipient of the mantle must therefore put himself in a "*prophetic process*" as there is a major shifting that repositions and realigns his spirit for divine elevation in the realm of the spirit.

The anointing and the mantle are complementary spiritual substances. They complement each other in that one receives an anointing and then graduates or develops it into a mantle. Therefore, you cannot talk of the mantle without first touching the realm of the anointing. Although they are of a different make up, gravity or intensity, their origin could always be traced back to the same source, hence some people use them interchangeably. They are both products or substances of God's glory. They are originally created from the glory of God but then tailor-made by spiritual laws and principles to suit a specific purpose.

Prophetically speaking, new mantles are falling on the earth in the same way manna fell from Heaven. Right now, there are mantles hovering over the Body of Christ, waiting to be released, and God is looking for those upon whom He can impart His mantle of power. Some mantles will resemble things we have seen before, while others will empower believers to do things that have never been done before. The Lord recently spoke to me where He showed me one of the mantles about to be released over the corporate Body of Christ. The Lord used the picture of Kathryn Kuhlman to symbolically speak to me that there is once again about to be released over the Church a mantle that is similar to the one this great woman of God wore. It is a Mantle of Glory and Creative Miracles. Not only will it release mass miracles, but it is deeply connected to our level of intimacy with the Person of the Holy Spirit. It is a mantle of extraordinary power as well as deep intimacy with God. This mantle releases creative miracles as the atmosphere of Heaven is released over our lives. This type of mantle will not just cover one or two. God wants to release it over the Corporate Body of Christ. God is looking for vessels He can endure with power out in the marketplace. We are about to witness an avalanche of "*backyard miracles*"- miracles taking place in the homes, workplaces, market places, out on the streets, in hospitals and in the malls. We will see creative miracles everywhere God's people go, just like the fall of dew every morning. But this mantle requires a lifestyle of deep communion with God and a life of complete surrender, obedience and death to self.

Moreover, one of the rare mantles that are being loosed right now upon the Body of Christ is the mantle of resurrection or raising the dead. Prophetically speaking, *new mantles of resurrection* are being loosed from the heavens upon the earth right now. There are mantles hovering over the Body of Christ, waiting to be released and God is looking for those who have developed a perennial hunger, insatiable appetite and unquenchable thirst for the supernatural and have enlarged their spiritual capacity to carry these mantles, so that He can place them on. These mantles will empower believers to do things that have never been done before. The Lord recently showed me one of the mantles about to be released over the corporate Body of Christ. The Lord used the picture of Smith Wigglesworth to symbolically speak to me that there is once again about to be released over the Church a mantle that is similar to the one this great man of God wore. It is a *Mantle of resurrection.* The Lord showed me that his anointing and ministry did not die when he passed into glory and that it would be resurrected if someone would just pick up his mantle that is lying on the earth. Not only will this mantle release the resurrection power to raise the dead but it will also release a greater manifestation of resurrection glory as the atmosphere of Heaven is released over the Corporate Body of Christ. There is therefore a vacancy in the Heavens as God is looking for vessels as candidates that He can endure with this resurrection mantle at the marketplace in this generation. The question is: Are you available to pick up the mantle?

A SEVENTH-FOLD DIVINE REVELATION OF THE MANTLE AND THE ANOINTING

Firstly, the mantle is for an office while the anointing is for service.

The anointing is specifically released upon an individual for service but the mantle is for an ordination or elevation into a specific office. The anointing is for general workers but the mantle is for office bearers. It is for this reason that the anointing can rest upon the multitudes but the mantle can rests upon a hand full of called, consecrated and devoted individuals. Secondly, the mantle is a permanent residence of power while the anointing temporarily comes and takes off once the work or divine tasks have been completed. The anointing rests upon a vessel and sometimes it takes off or gradually weans depending on the flow and usage but the mantle is permanently embedded on a man's spirit. Those who occupy a certain office like the prophetic office and seem to be moving in greater dimensions of power than others is actually because they are recipients of the mantle. So, the mantle establishes you. Do you know that you cannot be defined by the anointing upon your life because you can receive it today but tomorrow loose it? This is contrary to how the mantle operates because once you receive it, it anchors you and you can be easily identified with. The anointing is like a currency, it gravitates towards those with power but the mantle is like an academic credential that qualifies or certifies you to move in a certain realm in the spirit.

Secondly, the mantle is like a cloud and the anointing is like rain coming out of that cloud.

It is a fact that the mantle radiates the anointing. This means that you can get the anointing without a mantle but you can never get the mantle without the anointing because the mantle is an elevation or graduation of the anointing into a permanent office. This implies that you start by having an anointing, then as that anointing thickens, cements and solidifies as you go through tests and trials, then you can graduate into an office and a mantle can rest upon you. It is at this advanced stage in the realm of walking with God that the anointing changes from a liquid form into a solid, crystallised state - raw and undiluted. Philosophically speaking, a mantle could therefore be described as the *crystallisation or condensation of the anointing*. It is the anointing that has graduated into a superior quality in the realm of the spirit that ushers the recipient into an arena of divine exploits and enables him to command a greater degree of authority and power in the spirit realm than ever before. It is like a thick garment that eventually rests upon a man and catapults him into the realm of greatness. The mantle can therefore be described as the *official inauguration of the anointing.*

Thirdly, the mantle is limited in operation while the anointing is unlimited.

The impartation of the mantle is limited because it comes with much greater responsibility, accountability than the anointing. With the mantle, comes more power and greater responsibility and influence than the anointing. It's like a rob of a King which gives him more power to rule. That is why even when Elisha had the anointing which he received by virtue of association with his master Elijah the prophet, he still cried for the mantle at the departure of Elijah (1 Kings 19:19-21). In other words, the anointing was just not enough to get him to a place in the realm of the spirit where he wanted to be. Instead, he needed the mantle for a permanent move or ordination into the office of a prophet, hence he had to diligently seek for the mantle and it finally fell on him. In essence, the double portion of Elijah's spirit which Elisha desperately sought for is actually the *mantle* because the *mantle* is a double measure of the anointing that elevates someone into a higher, greater and deeper realm of authority and power in the realm of the spirit. That is why Elisha performed so many miracles after he got the mantle than before because with the mantle, comes more power, greater miracles, signs and wonders as well as mighty deeds.

Fourthly, the anointing produces fame or popularity while the mantle produces responsibility.

In today's church scenario, there are two types of Christians, that is, those who are running after the substance of the anointing and those who are seeking the mantle. The former move from one church conference to the next seeking for opportunities for impartation of the anointing while the former develops their characters and the quality of their spirit to reach a stage of maturity in the anointing. However, the mantle enables one to solidify his character and be established in the area of ministry. While the ones who is anointed demonstrates the power of God though miracles, signs and wonders in such a way that the world is able to see, the one who carries a mantle exudes the character and quality of Jesus. In other words, in the anointing, the people see the man but in the mantle, they see Jesus behind the man. The mantle carries a greater weight and scope of responsibility and accountability because it comes with greater authority. The one with the mantle can issues decrees over cities and national that would take effect for generations.

Fifthly, the mantle produces or births forth a greater manifesta-

tion of power, miracles, signs and wonders than the anointing.

If ever you want to see a heightened degree of miracles, signs and wonders being displayed through your hands, you need to grow in the mantle. This is why after receiving the mantle, Elisha was elevated into the greater depths of the miraculous than his peers. In other words, he automatically became their leader by virtue of the mantle. Sadly, many believers know the anointing but they do not know the mantle that produces that anointing. The anointing is like rain but the mantle is like a cloud that releases the rain. Have you ever wondered how the bones of Elisha raised a man from the dead more than 400 years after his death? While modern day preachers who exhibits an entry level understanding of the concepts of the anointing and mantle usually rant and rave behind the pulpit that the anointing had so socked into Elisha's body during his life time to the extent of permanently settling into his bones, the truth is that what raised the man from the dead as he came into contact with the bones of Elisha was not the anointing per se but the mantle. That was not the anointing in operation but the mantle at work. As a liquid spiritual substance, I don't think that the anointing would have lasted that long. I'm therefore of the opinion that it is actually the anointing that had rather graduated or solidified into a form hard and solid enough to dwell or persist in his bones even more than 400 years after his death. At the death of Elisha, the mantle, that jacket of power, "*the so called double portion of the spirit*" which rested upon Elisha when his master Elijah was taken to Heaven by chariots of fire, is what had settled upon him even unto the grave.

Sixthly, while people can receive the anointing from other human vessels, you can actually pick up the mantle from the surface of the earth or its very atmosphere

It must be understood that although the anointing is restricted in terms of its administration, for example, you receive an anointing form another human vessel but in the case of the mantle, the laws that govern its administration are different in that you can also pick it up from the surface of the earth or from the very atmosphere where it was ministered years back. Just like the mantle of Elisha that rested on the surface of the earth, there are mantles that have lingered, persisted or remained on the surface on the earth unclaimed and are waiting for believers to take them up. Do you notice that not only did the man who came into contact with the bones of Elisha rise up from the dead but he also picked up the mantle. Many believers when they read this scripture, they only see the man coming into contact with Elisha's bones and rising up from the dead but if you read it with the eyes of the spirit, you will see the man picking up the mantle. Do you know that the one who comes into contact with an exposed electric power, not only does he gets electrocuted but he also carries the electric flow into his very own body. So, the man received a double dose by rising form the dead and also picking up the mantle.

Lastly, the mantle is evidently a sign of divine elevation or promotion in the realm of the spirit

How does a minister know whether he/he has been promoted or elevated to a higher position or dimension of authority in the realm of the spirit? The most precise way is by looking at the extent to which the mantle has solidified or broadened. The mantle is evidently a sign of divine elevation or promotion in the spirit because with the mantle comes greater, authority, leadership and territorial governance. It happens that over the course of time, one gets promoted by God in the spirit and the mantle serve as a proof of such level of divine elevation. So, while the anointing advertises you as a minister, the mantle anchors or establishes you. It a pity that many people remains at the level where their gifts are being advertised and they never graduate to a position where they are anchored in the spirit realm

TYPES OF MANTLES

It must be understood that the tasks or nature of assignments in the kingdom are diverse, hence as much as there are different types of anointing that serve different purposes, there are also different mantles which are divinely orchestrated for different purposes. There are multitudes of different types of mantles in the kingdom. For example, there is a mantle for *breakthrough,* a mantle for *finances or wealth,* a mantle for *revelation* and the mantle for *governance,* mantle for *miracles, mantle for deliverance,* mantle for *evangelism, teaching, pastoral, apostolic and prophetic mantle,* mantle for *healing,* mantle for *prosperity,* mantle for *worship and so forth.* For revelation purposes, these myriad of mantles can be categorised into *Generational mantles, Special* or *Peculiar mantles* and

New or End time Mantles.

Generational Mantles

These are relationship based mantles which are transferred or imparted from the previous generation through spiritual fatherhood and son ship.

They are imparted by spiritual fathers, mothers or mentors upon their spiritual sons and daughters and cause them to operate in the same dimension of power or miraculous as them. This is one of the ways through which the treasure of God's anointing is preserved throughout generations. Their manifestation comes through a mentor–disciple or teacher-student, master–servant hood relationships. For example, Joshua received a generational mantle from Moses and David received one from Saul. The most quintessential example of a generational mantle is the one that Elisha received from Elijah as recorded in 1 Kings 19:19. Sadly, some folks when they read this portion of the scripture, they only see a sash, or piece of cloth dropping off from Elijah and landing upon Elisha but the truth is that it was not just a piece of cloth. It was a mantle. This mantle actually was a symbol of divine elevation into that particular office. It showed that the Holy Spirit was coming upon Elisha, but it wasn't the actual anointing itself but a thicker spiritual substance. It was a symbol of the mantle of God's power.

In our generation, it is said that Benny Hinn received a mantle from Kathrine Khulman. However, it must be expressly understood that generational mantles are not only restricted or confined to spiritual relationships but to natural ones as well. They can be transferred from natural fathers to their natural sons. For example, Kenneth Hagin Jr. received mantle from his father Kenneth Hagin and Joel Austin received a mantle from his father John Osteen.

Special or Peculiar Mantles

Special miracles are peculiar mantles that are released or given by God directly from Heaven upon men and women to carry out a specific mandate or accomplish specific tasks in a generation.

It is a spiritual fact that one can never bankrupt God's source of provision. While under normal circumstances, people usually wait to receive the mantles from the previous generation, God does not wait for His servants to die so that He could impart the mantles on the next generation. Instead, there are special mantles that are released on the earth, not upon everybody but upon certain vessels, chosen through the sovereignty of God to carry a mantle of power in a generation. The major characteristic feature of a special mantle is that it enables an individual to excel or function at a level that is by far higher than others in the Kingdom. For example, in our generation, highly anointed men of God who seem to be excelling in miracles of healing, deliverance, prophecy or in any other grace at a level higher than others, have actually received these *special mantles*. Special mantles are peculiar in nature and degree of manifestation. These are given on the basis of God's sovereignty and choice, hence cannot be questioned, contended or queried. They are given by God and placed directly upon certain vessels to carry out a specific mandate in a particular generation. Once the purpose is carried out, the mantle cannot be duplicated. It must be noted that while human life is limited to a life span, the mantle is not limited, hence upon the death of a vessel; it is transferred to the next generation.

In the Bible, Joseph's garment of many colours is a quintessential example and portrait of a mantle in the natural realm. While the majority of believers hold a general notion that Joseph's garment of many colours represents favour, the greater truth is that it actually speaks of favour in the area of spiritual covering of the mantle. It was a foretaste of the mantle of governance which was destined to fall upon Joseph in Egypt. In the natural realm, while it appeared to be just a nice, unique garment, in the spirit realm, that was actually a mantle of wealth, authority and governance. It's definitely not coincidence that Joseph's father designed it that way because as a man of God, he was led by the Spirit to establish a spiritual destiny for the whole of Israel though his own son.

In the similar fashion in which Jacob designed a garment of many colours for his son, Joseph, God is also releasing special mantle upon his servants. As much as God gives a special or peculiar anointing to His servants, He also ordains a special mantle upon those whom He has chosen to undertake specific tasks in the kingdom. For example, David received a special mantle for praise and worship which made him to excel in that area more than any other person. Smith Wiggles Worth was given a special mantle to raise the dead, hence he excelled in that area of ministry more than everyone in his generation. William Braham was given also a special mantle of healing to such an extent that germs which came into contact with his body died instantly under the observation of medical doctors. The truth of the matter is that when a special mantle is given, God will often give you a preview of what to expect in the ministry as long as we persevere and remain faithful up to the end.

New/ Seasonal/ End Time Mantles

These are prophetic mantles which God has reserved for the end time dispensation to fall upon a distinct breed of believers who shall hunger and thirst for the move of God in this critical season.

These have not been released before in the days gone by but are new and fresh from the Throne Room of Heaven. Do you remember when God spoke through the voice of Isaiah in Isaiah 48:7 saying, *Behold, I'm doing a new thing! They are created now, and not so long ago, you have not heard of them before today, so you cannot say, "Yes, I knew them*", part of this new thing is actually the release of the end time mantles as a brand new phenomenon unfolding directly from God's Throne. When an army general retires, his uniform is not discarded but he surrenders it to the authorities which would then be won by somebody else joining the air force. As it is in the natural, so it is in the spirit. It must be understood that in terms of usage, there are *used mantles* which were used by men of God in the generations gone by and are now available for the next generation to pick them up so that they are able to do the same task and move in the same dimension of power as the previous generation. Then there are *torn mantles* which have been abused or wrongly used by people who received them and did not walk in the faithfulness of their callings. Then there are *new mantles* which are brand new mantles or jackets of power which God is dropping directly from the Throne Room upon His servants for the accomplishment of certain divine tasks in these end times. These have never been used or won by anybody in the previous generation. Instead, they shall fall in larger and greater quality and quantity, taking into account a myriad of divine tasks that has to be completed in the Kingdom. By reason of the end time season, anyone who avails himself for the work of ministry becomes a candidate or recipient of such mantles. When God declared in 1 Corinthians 2:9-10that, "*No eye have seen, nor ear heard nor has it entered into the heart of man what God has prepared for those who love Him*", He actually spoke of the new mantles that He has prepared to fall upon His servants for an end time harvest, which nobody has seen, heard, comprehended or witnessed in the history of humanity.

Prophetically speaking, there are mantles that have been loosed on earth right now including some that have never been seen before. Some are abandoned mantles which were supposed to fall upon some people but they were not readily available to take them up at the time of their release. Some were rejected and never accepted by the recipients who died due to lack of revelation and love of the world. There are apostolic and prophetic mantles, teaching, pastoral and evangelical mantles, worship mantles, spiritual warfare mantles, governmental mantles, leadership mantles and so forth. All these mantles are therefore awaiting God's people to pick them up and use them to expand the kingdom. Therefore, if you could only avail yourself to be used by God in this end time season, you are likely to be a candidate for mantles of this nature to fall on you.

SEVEN SPIRITUAL PRINCIPLES OF RECEIVING AND RELEASING THE MANTLE

1. *Impartation*

Impartation takes place due to a direct intervention or contact between your spirit and the Holy Spirit. The mantle comes from God to man but impartation is given from one man to another by God's will. Paul says, "*Brethren, I long to see you, that I may impart some spiritual gift*". However, you must understand that it is not only spiritual gifts that can be imparted but the mantle as well. God takes or transfers the mantle from an anointed individual upon those who desperately seek it. Impartation produces similarity between the giver and the recipient of the mantle. Impartation comes through laying of hands, reading anointed books, listening to powerful teachings, preaching, God's word, prophesies, clothes and so forth. We therefore receive an impartation when we capture the spirit of the mantle. Therefore, if you desperately need a mantle, then rigorously pursue the above mentioned ways through which you can receive an impartation.

2. *Association or Sphere of influence*

There are mantles that rest upon vessels by virtue of sphere of influence, association, affiliation, partnership or belonging. The law of contagious experience or association implies that one can actually pick up a mantle from a territory. This mantle comes by fellowshipping in a particular ministry, closely following spiritual programs of a man of God, partnership with a ministry, influence through television, ministry products such as DVDs, taps, books or any other divine material. That is why you find that people who serve under a particular man of God are able to flow in the same anointing or mantle as him. This is because the anointing of God is highly contagious, hence by coming under a spiritual covering though association, it is transferred. Elisha received the mantle from Elijah by virtue of association or contagious experience. Therefore, if you need the mantle through this way, then get closer to a man of God or ministry which God has anointed.

I recall vividly how I received a mantle of power from Pastor Chris. I followed the man closely and regularly watched him on TV and made it appoint not to miss any of his international conferences. It happened that on a given day, God showed me a vision in which I saw Pastor Chris holding a bunch of keys. He then threw the bunch of keys straight at me and as soon as I caught them with both my hands, my physical countenance changed such that I looked exactly like him. When I regained my consciousness, I had literally received the mantle of power and instantly I was elevated into a higher realm in the realm of the spirit, evidenced by a greater demonstration of power at the same level that Pastor Christ was operating. That is why at times when I preach, people see Pastor Chris because of the mantle that I received from him.

3. ***Placing a demand on the mantle***

It must be expressly understood that with or without our consciousness, there are spiritual exchanges or divine transactions that takes place in the realm of the spirit in the area of ministry. Such comes by faith, giving, sowing seeds or even making sacrifices. For example, to receive a mantle from a man of God, you can buy him a notable gift and the mantle will rest upon you depending on how connected you are. After releasing that seed or sacrifice, one can then place a demand on the mantle. Placing a demand speaks of a spiritual connection to a source of the mantle but one has to understand the spiritual laws and principles involved to produce expected results. Placing a demand on the mantle means to express a deep desire or hunger for the supernatural manifestation of God's power that is upon a vessel.

Ceteris paribus, a demand is placed by *faith*. When you place a demand on a minister, your faith is pulling the manifestation resident in their spirit. For example, if a minister is ministering and suddenly stops to call someone with a particular condition, it is because that person has placed a demand in the spirit realm. However, at times these spiritual transactions or placing a demand takes place without necessarily sacrificing or sowing a seed but by the degree of openness of one's spirit to receive the mantle. The mantle is the weight or heaviness of the covering of the anointing resting upon a vessel, hence the vessel's carrying capacity must be enlarged or widened for the mantle to rest upon him. For example, if one places a demand on the mantle but his spirit is not fully developed or rightly positioned, he might not receive the fall of the mantle. When someone becomes too familiar with a man of God, it becomes difficult to place a demand on the mantle due to familiarity. When someone does not place a demand on the mantle, he stops being a recipient of that mantle.

4. *Spiritual Sonship*

There are mantles that fall upon individuals as a result of their continued, persistent faithfulness in serving a man of God from the previous generation. Taking into account the spiritual law and principle that men of God do not depart to Heaven with their mantles, they would have to impart them upon their spiritual sons for continuity of their ministries and visions of God. However, it must be made expressly clear that you don't have to wait for a man of God to die before you could receive his mantle. You can access other avenues of receiving the mantle while still enjoying his presence. That is why it is advisable that every believer should have a spiritual mentor because there are certain things which God might not give you directly but might deposit them on spiritual fathers so that sons and daughters could easily make a spiritual withdrawal from them.

5. *Tapping into higher realms of Glory*

Fervently, persistently and meticulously seeking after God's glory by staying in His presence is one of the key strategies to provoking a fall of a mantle. Note that the mantle is not only formed due to the progressive build-up of the substance of the anointing but it is also a product of the glory of God. For example, when the glory of God rests upon a human vessel, it elevates him to a higher dimension of authority and also increases greater demonstrations of power. That is why there is such a thing called the *mantle of the glory*. This is a result of a heightened degree of accumulation of glory upon a vessel such that it becomes a permanent or integral aspect of one's life.

Moses had a thick mantle for miracles, signs and wonders because the glory of God had rubbed intensely on him to such an extent that *his face was shining and the children of Israel could not look at him* (Exodus 34:29-35). That is why he was able to transfer this mantle of glory upon Joshua and the seventy elders. Prophet Elijah had a prophetic mantle because he continuously stood in the presence of God such that the glory of God that rested upon him was so strong that it permeated every core of his being. That is why he was able to pass that mantle to Elisha in the next generation. The double portion of Elijah's spirit is actually the mantle. Therefore, if you desperately need the mantle to fall upon you, rather than growing in the anointing or receiving it from somebody else through impartation, another option is to directly absorb, God's glory and the glory will rain a mantle upon your life. This is because the mantle is a product of God's glory, hence by staying more in the presence of God's glory, one can position himself as a candidate or recipient of the mantle because with the glory comes the mantle. That is why in the current dispensation, more emphasis in the church should be placed on the transition from the realm of the anointing to the realm of glory because it is the glory that directly gives birth to mantles.

6. *Progressive graduation in the realm of the anointing*

There is such a thing called *the mantle of the anointing*. This is a type of mantle that results from the build-up process or accumulation of volumes of measureless anointing upon an individual. The anointing reaches a point whereby it chrysalises and becomes a thick covering or a permanent dwelling in the spirit of a vessel. When it finally solidifies and turns into this thick covering, it is no longer just an ordinary anointing but a mantle of the anointing. Therefore if you need a mantle, grow in the anointing or develop the anointing that you have already received and it will solidify into a mantle. It is therefore apparent that besides receiving a mantle through impartation, one of the methods of reception is to progressively graduate or migrate from the first dimension, through the second dimension until an atmosphere of the mantle builds up upon your life in the third dimension.

7. *Divine location by grace and connectivity to God's favour*

It is a greater truth that the law of grace supersedes all spiritual laws of God. Hence, there is a mantle that one can receive from God, not because he has done anything amazing but just because he has been located by grace and bestowed favour. This is the same way by which Joseph was given a garment of many colours by his father in the midst of his brothers (Genesis 37:2-11). The garment of many colours was the *symbolic of a mantle.* In her biography, Katherine Khulman reveals that the mantle that she received was originally meant for two other people but just because they did not fully meet the divine qualifications in terms of the standard of life which God had ordained for their callings, the mantle finally rested upon her. This means even if she was not the first preference or the preferred candidate of reception of the anointing through the law of grace, God located her and the mantle eventually fell upon her. This is another way through which some can get to receive the mantle. Therefore, don't be shocked to see people that you never thought God could use them, receive the mantle. It is by GRACE that they got it.

CHAPTER FOUR

THE FOURTH DIMENSION:

THE DIMENSION OF THE PRESENCE

The presence represents a radiation or refection of God's glory. It is the manifest touch that comes when the glory of God is radiated in a particular place . The presence is not the glory but the radiation or refection of that glory. It is a signal that God is in the house. Basically, the anointing of God is a manifestation of the power of God while the glory of God is a manifestation of His attributes. However, the power of God and the presence of God are inseparable because God does not demonstrate His power without His presence. Jesus said, *"When the Holy Spirit has come upon you (His presence), you shall receive power (His anointing of power* (Acts 1:8). Mark 16:17 reads – And these signs (His power) shall follow those who believe in My Name (His presence). In the case of Elijah's encounter with God, on Mount Horeb, what shook the mountains apart, brought forth an earthquake and a boisterous wind was a display of the power of God but His presence was not there (1 Kings 19:11-13). This is because the power of God is displayed through manifestation but the presence comes with the glory. In the absence of a manifestation, there is no power but the presence can come without a manifestation.

In the realm of the spirit, we carry different measures and degrees of God's presence. There is a *general omni- presence* and a *manifest presence.* The general presence is a common outer court presence that manifest everywhere by the grace of God. On the other hand, the manifest presence is a specific and tangible presence that comes or originates straight from the throne room and is manifested intensely when God is moving or doing something special in a service. It is the manifest presence that brings about healings, deliverance, miracles, signs and wonders. You can just be in the presence of God and you could just press deeper and deeper with greater hunger for more of the presence of God. And as the presence of God and the glory of God increases in your life, it is just like putting fertilizer into the ground into the seed that is growing and it just blossoms.

It is possible for one to be under the atmosphere of God's presence 24 hours as long as the right atmosphere is activated. The presence of God has to be practised, stirred, activated, invoked or invigorated. That is why there is such a thing called *practising the presence.* It is in the presence of God that we get so refreshed, revitalised, rejuvenated and invigorated with divine energy. Luke, one of the writers of the Bible, let us know in Acts 3:19 that *we should repent so that the times of refreshing came come from the presence of the Lord.* This supernatural infusion is like a breath of fresh air that will invigorate you and position you for exploits on the Kingdom. It must be understood expressly that while God generally breeds His presence in measures and degrees, there is a part that you should play in order to usher His presence. Hence, there is no such thing as an automatic presence. Instead, it has to be stirred through such spiritual acts as having a constant flow of music, practical involvement in ministerial sessions, listening to powerful sermons, studying the word as well as prayer and fasting. That is what we call *the practice of God's presence.*

THE THREE DEGREES OF GOD'S PRESENCE

It must be understood that while God fills all His creation by His presence and is intricately infused in the fabric of His creation, the extent to which He manifest Himself across the universe is not the same. There are 3 degrees of God's presence unveiled in the word of God. These degrees depict the extent to which the presence of God is manifested in a certain locality. The first is the *abiding presence* which is the general presence that prevails over all creation. The second is the *manifested or revealed presence* which is a tangible presence that is activated through prayer, fasting, reading the word and engagement in other spiritual exercises. Then the third is the *transforming presence* which prevails when He transforms your physical body because of the height of His presence.

1. The Abiding Presence

This is the first degree of manifestation of God's presence in every fabric of His creation. It is unveiled in John 14:20 where Jesus said *in that day you will know that I am in my Father, and you in me, and I in you.* This is called His *abiding presence.* It is the consciousness of His presence. Another scriptural reference that depicts the abiding presence is when Jesus said, "*Where 2 or 3 are gathered in my name there am I in the midst of them.*" This revelation comes out clearly when you cross reference to Matthew 28:20, whereby Jesus said, "*I am with you always, to the close of the age*". That is just His general abiding presence. Every born again Christian has that. Salvation brings to you His abiding presence in our heart. You don't need Ephesians 3 to be born again for it speaks about Jesus dwelling in our hearts for which Paul is praying for. He is not talking about being born again. He is talking about another type of presence. The first presence is that abiding presence that all of us receive when we were born again. We know Jesus came into our hearts. We sense the peace in our hearts. He abides in us.

1. The Manifested Presence

But there is another presence that we can classify as the *manifested presence.* To substantiate this revelation with scriptural evidence, Jesus said in John 14:21 *He who has My commandments and keeps them, he it is who loves Me; and he who loves Me will be loved by my Father, and I will love him and manifest myself to him.* Obviously He is talking about a different presence. He is not talking about every Christian. He is talking about he who keeps His commandments which represents His word. There are a lot of Christians who don't fully keep His word. They are born again no doubt. They have a certain measure of His presence. What do they not have? They don't have the Ephesians 3 presence. They don't have the answer to Paul's prayer in Ephesians 3. Paul prayed that *Christ may dwell in their hearts in all fullness that they may comprehend the height, the length, the width, the depth of the love of Christ and be filled with the fullness of God.* They don't have His manifested presence. Once you are born again, there is a peace in your heart, a joy in your heart that is always there unless you fall into sin. And yet when you spend time praying or spend extra time with God, perhaps in your prayer closet another presence comes. You know He is there yet He is even there stronger. What is that presence? It is His manifested presence. His presence that is thicker and stronger at the second level. That is Ephesians 3 and 4 presence.

To tap into the manifested presence, you need to build on word of God (*Kratos*) and the indwelling presence of the Holy Spirit (*Ischus*). Spend time meditating on the Word and have a strong devotional life and prayer. And you build it to a certain point where the manifested presence comes and starts working. And as you reach a certain point, you began to touch on *exousia* and *dunamis.* You are now at the second level having the manifested presence. Every time you enter into prayer the presence of God is there.

2. The Transforming Presence

But there is another third presence that is even greater. In John 14:22, Judas (not Iscariot) said to Jesus, "*Lord, how is it that you will manifest yourself to us, and not to the world?* Jesus answered him, "*If a man loves me, he will keep My Word, and my Father will love him, and we will come to him and make our home with him.* That's the third and most powerful presence that very few people fully experience. Do you notice that 2 verses back Jesus said I will manifest to him but .now He says we will come to him and make our home with him? This third degree of God's presence is the *transforming presence* which manifests when He transforms your physical body because of the height of His presence.

If you live in the transforming presence constantly you know what will happen? You will have to be translated just like Enoch it's so powerful. And that's the level that Paul is talking about in chapter 5 of Ephesians. At this level, you reach a point where you are filled with the Spirit all the time. In chapter 1 and 2 of Ephesians, he is preparing you to be habitation of God. In chapter 3 and 4, he is talking about being rooted in Christ and growing up in Christ. But not everyone knows how to pray into the manifested presence of God. That's why we are teaching the Word. We first learn the secrets of *kratos* and *ischus.* But then when we began to learn *proseuche* and *deesis* and bring in *exousia* and *dunamis* we began to take a bigger and higher step into the transforming presence. You remember what happened in Numbers 16 and 17. The Israelites were quarrelling about who will be their leader. And they didn't accept Aaron as a priest. And God said all you 12 tribes each one of you give me a rod. And I will put that rod in God's presence and in the morning you will see who God chooses. The next morning Aaron's rod a stick that is dead. I mean Moses had been using that rod for a long time. But in the presence of God the transforming presence the dead shall live again. And the wood came alive. The wood bore leaves and flowers. And the next morning they saw a fresh new almond. Even in the natural if it is a live rod it is also impossible because plants don't grow over night and don't bear fruit overnight. This is something else. What is that? It is the transforming presence.

To substantiate this revelation with further scriptural evidence, when Moses came down from the mountain the second time with the 2 new tablets. There was something different. He saw God's glory. And in Exodus 33 he said God show me your glory. And God showed him His glory and Moses' face shine like a light bulb. The Bible says his skin radiated with beams of God's glory. That's called the *transforming glory*. Paul talks about this degree of presence in 2 Corinthians. *As we behold Him we are transformed and changed to the same image.* The third is the transforming glory. When God the Father and the Son reach a point where they abide with us you will begin to understand that the heavenly presence is now here. The same presence of the Father is in us. There are 3 things about God, Omnipotent - He is all-powerful, Omniscience - He is all knowing and Omnipresence - He is everywhere. Omnipresence is not just God is everywhere but is everywhere equally. In other word His presence don't have to be stronger here and weaker there. Sadly He cannot do that all the time because the avenues and laws that work His presence are not followed by men and women.

Conclusively, in chapter 1 and 2 of Ephesians, Paul is talking about the abiding presence. Learning how to remain seated in the heavenly place. That is His abiding presence. In chapter 3 and 4 he is talking about His manifested presence. Now when He manifest there is a natural result. That is why there is an anointing upon. He prayed in Eph. 3 for the manifested presence to come forth. In chapter 5 and 6 he is talking about His transforming presence. We are His flesh and His bones. And the reality of that must sink into our life. We are so filled with His Spirit that what comes out is only psalms, hymns and spiritual songs. In chapter 4 he was still trying to get them not to say the wrong thing. Don't let any corrupt communication come out, don't quench the Spirit, don't grieve the Spirit. But in chapter 5 he doesn't talk about grieving or corrupt communication that's in the past. Now he talks about the psalms and the hymns coming out because you are so full of God. That when you speak it's God's Word coming out through your life. You are so transformed that your physical body becomes His. That is Luke 9 as He prayed His body and His garments were changed and transformed. That is His transforming presence. We need to understand the combination of both those things.

CHAPTER FIVE

THE FIFTH DIMENSION:

The Dimension of the Miraculous

A DIVINE REVELATION OF HOW TO OPERATE IN THE REALM OF THE MIRACULOUS

An introductory perspective to the realm of the miraculous

In an endeavour to establish a profound and holistic understanding of the realm of the supernatural, it is of paramount importance that we provide an introductory perspective to the realm of the miraculous as a foundational principle to illustrate how the supernatural realm operates, functions or is governed. The Apostle Paul places a nugget of truth right into our hands and thus ushering us into the realm of the miraculous when he affirms in 2 Corinthians 12:12 that,

Surely, the signs of an apostle were accomplished amongst you with all perseverance in

signs and wonders and mighty deeds.

Note that our opening scripture above brings to light the "*Signs*" of the apostolic office. That means Apostles as ordained by God, are the Biblical forerunners and pioneers of the miraculous realm. For clarity of purpose, let us cross reference to another scripture in Acts 2:22 which describes *"Jesus as a man approved by God in miracles signs and wonders and mighty deeds"*. This tells me that miracles, signs, wonders and mighty deeds are what validated and authenticated the ministry of Jesus while on earth. It is worth noting that in the realm of the miraculous; Jesus is our yardstick or benchmark by which we measure our standard of operating in the supernatural. Jesus functioned in all the four dimensions in the realm of the miraculous, hence His ministry was a torrent of miracles that inspired awe and wonder in the multitudes who witnessed them. To substantiate the notion that Jesus functioned in all these dimensions of the miraculous, when asked by John's disciples whether He was the Messiah or not in, He responded by saying,

"*Go and tell John the things which you see, the dead are raised, the lepers are cleansed, the crippled walk, devils are cast out and the poor in spirit has the word preached to them* (Luke 7:22).

This tells me that within these dimensions of the realm of the miraculous are an array or acts of divine exploits such as the ones enumerated in the above scripture. These come as an impartation of divine power from the Holy Spirit as He has now delegated His mission to believers by giving us the same and even higher dimension of supernatural power Jesus had exhibited on earth so that we too can perform miracles, signs and wonders and mighty deeds in our generation. Notable is the realisation that every man ordained by God into the fivefold ministerial office seem to be operating in all these *four dimensions* of supernatural power. This implies that all the incredible happenings recorded in the Bible from Genesis to Revelation can be categorised into *miracles, signs, wonders and mighty deeds* and these are key dimensions in the realm of the miraculous. This leads us to an inevitable conclusion that in the realm of the miraculous, there are **FOUR** main dimensions, depths, degrees and levels and these are, **No. 1 *Miracles*, No. 2 *Signs* and No. 3 *Wonders* and No. 4 *Mighty deeds*.**

Owing to a lack of revelation, it is a typical scenario in the Body of Christ that many people use the phrase *"signs and wonders"* as an umbrella term for all kinds of supernatural displays of power and consider miracles, a large subset of such events, usually objectively observable. To provide divine correction and clarity on this matter, let's highlight the distinguishable characteristics of these realms of the miraculous. Firstly, a sign is defined in Greek as a mark or token that distinguishes and authenticates divine activity and points people to God. Put differently, it's an object, quality or event whose presence or occurrence indicates the probable presence or occurrence of something else. Secondly, a wonder is a spectacular, fascinating, enthralling and hilarious spiritual experience, encounter or occurrence that causes a beholder to marvel in astonishment or admiration. Thirdly, a miracle is an incredible happening, phenomenon, occurrence or unusual manifestation that takes place as a result of sudden divine intervention of God in the affairs of humanity. Lastly, a mighty deed is a manifestation of the supernatural power of God in extreme cases and radical situations where human comprehension and reasoning cannot suffice. These four words often function interchangeably. However, other signs and wonders that might not be classified as miracles could include more subjective supernatural experiences such as dreams, visions, trances, angel encounters, and prophetic words of knowledge.

It is worth exploring the divine truth that signs and wonders have a two-fold implication – they carry both meaning and awe, revelation and fascination. They are the most prolific means of communication between the God of Heaven and humankind as God speaks through a sign and a wonder Signs and wonders carry a sincere depth of meaning, message and revelation coupled with astonishment, amazement and awe. Signs and wonders directed from the throne will have both revelation and marvel intermingled as one. I have never seen God perform a wonder of any sort without an applied message, meaning or purpose.

KEY REALMS IN THE DIMENSION OF THE MIRACULOUS

The Realm of Miracles.

It is of paramount importance in a view to enhance a significant level of understanding of the realm of the miraculous that we make reference to Greek and Hebrew terminology so that we could understand divine concepts in their original context. The word miracle is derived from the Greek word, *"Dynamis",* which means an inherent or latent power, ability or strength residing in an object by virtue of its nature. In a practical sense, a miracle is therefore defined as follows:

It is an incredible happening, occurrence or unusual manifesta-

tion that takes place in the natural realm as a result of a sudden divine intervention of God in the affairs of humanity to the extent that it cannot be fathomed or comprehended by human reasoning and intellectual ability. In an endeavour to present a more clearer and practical description of the concept, a miracle could also be defined as an instantaneous manifestation of God's tangible and visible supernatural power in the normal course of an individual's life, with a consequence of defying the natural laws of time, space and matter.

In essence, when a situation has reached a point of impossibility that warrants divine intervention and man finds himself in a place where medicine and science cannot help and through the name of Jesus, there is a visible, tangible and instantaneous change in the situation, that is said to be a *miracle.* Miracles are always traced to divinity, hence any natural phenomenon, regardless of the magnitude of its occurrence, cannot be attributable or qualified as a miracle. It is only when the realm of the spirit is revealed or manifested in the natural realm such that there is a defiance in the laws of nature that a miracle is said to have transpired.

However, although miracles may be daily occurrences in the spirit realm, they are uncommon in the realm of natural and that is why they are called *miracles.* It must be understood therefore that in the realm of the spirit, there is no such thing as a miracle since everything is perfectly divine. For instance, in Heaven, there are no sick, crippled or dead people because of the atmosphere of glory. However, whenever something is brought from the spirit world to the natural world, it amazes people because it is not usual in the natural realm. In the spirit world, it might not amaze anybody by virtue of the frequency of its occurrence. For example, if Michael the Arch Angel brings down the devil by sword in the spirit world, that is not regarded as a miracle because it is a daily occurrence that devils are busted and thrashed in the spirit world. However, if Apostle Frequency Revelator casts out a demon from a man in the natural world, that becomes a miracle because it is not a daily occurrence in that realm. A miracle can be something small as long as its manifestation is not common in the natural world.

Miracles are gravity defying and logic breaking scenarios in the natural realm. In other words, they defy the laws of nature and break the normal cycle of logic and reasoning. For instance, in the natural realm, the law of gravity states that if you throw a stone upwards, it will always come down. If by whatever means you throw a stone up into the atmosphere and it doesn't crash back onto the ground, then it is a miracle because it is an uncommon or unusual manifestation in the natural realm. This is the reason why walking on water is a miracle because it defies the natural laws of gravity. That is why those who live in the spirit realm, certain things that shock ordinary people in the natural world do not amaze them because they are daily experiences in the spirit realm in which they operate. It must also be understood that God responds to your faith and not your situation, He does not live in the realm of pity but He lives in the realm of faith hence a miracle is brought into manifestation either by faith, revelation or power.

TYPES OF MIRACLES

As much as there are divergent dimensions in the realm of miraculous, there are also different types of miracles which believers in the Body of Christ could perform in the name of Jesus Christ. These depict a flavour or unique manifestation of different aspects of God's power. These are 1. *Ordinary miracles* 2. *Unusual or special miracles* and 3. *Creative miracles.* It is important to note that the categorisation of these miracles is defined or determined by their nature of occurrence, degree of intensity of manifestation and the impact they have on their recipients. It is therefore not my solemn intention to create a doctrine around this subject but to provide guidelines that will reinforce a significant level of understanding of these divine concepts.

1. *Ordinary or Common miracles*

These are commonly shared miracles that take place during the ordinary course of life as a result of believing in the name of Jesus. Many of the miracles performed in the Bible fall in this category. They are ordinary in the sense that they have been commonly and repeatedly performed by many people in generations past such that their manifestation or performance does no longer amaze humanity to a larger extent.

These are usually miracles of healing for example, healing the sick from various diseases such as cancer, debates, TB, casting out demons, cleansing lepers or opening of the eyes of the blind.

They are said to be ordinary not in the sense that they are of a natural origin or lesser in significance but considering the greater depths and dimensions of power available in the realm of the supernatural, they are the entry level in the realm of the miraculous. They are ordinary, not by human standards but from God's perspective, as far as Jesus is concerned. For example, when Jesus proclaimed in John 14:12 that, *"Greater things than these shall you do"*, the term *"these"*, refers to the common miracles of the Bible. Therefore, Jesus actually meant that believers would migrate from this level of common miracles to a higher realm of creative miracles and unusual miracles.

The truth is that common miracles are a divine legitimate birth right and an irrevocable inheritance of every believer; hence they can be performed by anybody as long as they believe in the name of Jesus. They are unveiled by Jesus's declaration in Mark 16:17-18 that,

These signs shall follow those who believe. In My name, they shall cast out devils, they shall pick up serpents with their tails, when they lay hands on the sick, and the sick shall recover, when they eat anything deadly, it shall by no means hurt them".

The above scripture therefore defines the essence of what common miracles are. These are common miracles because they are a common standard by which every believer must operate at. This implies that anybody who claims to believe in Jesus Christ should be able to move in the dimension of these ordinary miracles. In most cases while ordinary people are amazed by common miracles, in actual fact they are not supposed to be treated with awe at all because as far as Jesus is concerned, these are basic entry level experiences in the spirit realm, hence must be regarded as daily or common experiences in the Body of Christ.

2. *Unusual or Special Miracles*

A special miracle is a kind of manifestation that is peculiar, uncommon, and unusual to ordinary life and its manifestation in the realm of God's power is such that it doesn't flow all the time but manifest whenever God does something special in a specific season.

There are special manifestations of God's supernatural power that are uncommon or unusual in the natural realm or to a generation. They are said to be unusual miracles in the sense that they are not a common experience, they don't manifest every day or all the time and they are not experienced by everybody. They are special operations and manifestations of the Spirit. Secondly, they are said to be unusual or special miracles in the sense that their manifestation requires a special grace to perform them. It must be understood in this regard that every believer is anointed to some degree in accordance with God's will and to the level that they are willing to be used by God. However, God does grant special abilities or anointing to certain individuals who seem to be able to operate in a higher degree of various gifts than others. These are *special anointings* or operations granted through God's sovereignty upon whichever vessel He chooses and they are not something that someone can just simply call upon at their own discretion (1Corinthians12:11). Such *special anointings* produces new and special manifestations and operations that are unique, peculiar and uncommon to a generation. These are called *special miracles.*

Their manifestation is evident in Acts 19:11 which testifies that,

> *God wrought unusual miracles by the hands of Paul such that aprons and handkerchiefs were taken from his body and laid on the sick and they were healed and evil spirits departed from them.*

In view of the scripture above, it suffices to say that the only time the word "*special*" is used in the New Testament is in relation to the special miracles that God wrought by the hands of the apostle Paul. What made these miracles *"special"* is that they were unique one time occurrences and from the Biblical record, this was the only time something like this ever happened in the ministry of Paul. This was much like Peter's shadow in Acts 5:15, whereby the sick were brought out into the streets and laid on coaches so that at least the shadow of Peter passing by might fall on them. Note that it's not every time that the sick were healed by Peter's shadow. This was a *special operation* which the Holy Spirit orchestrated at that specific time. Other special miracles of the Bible are: Jesus walking on water and Joshua commanding the sun to go backwards since it wasn't every time that believers staged a modelling show or marching parade on the sea and it wasn't a daily occurrence that the sun was stopped but it's something that happened once in a life time.

It is worth exploring the divine truth that special miracles are a major characteristic feature of the end time dispensation; hence they are reserved only for those who will tap into higher realms of glory and the greater depths of the miraculous to believe God for the impossible. It is evident across a broad spectrum of Christian faith in our generation that there are key individuals who seem to operate in certain areas with a greater anointing than others.

Again, this is something that God anoints them to do for a specific reason and it is not something that we, on our own can just scoop up at will. To illustrate this divine truth with reference to a quintessential example, a man called Smith Wigglesworth was given a special anointing and used by God in a special ministry of raising the dead. It is said that the man moved mightily in the realm of the miraculous to the extent that he would not allow anyone from his neighbourhood to die or depart from this earth without his permission. Moreover, God also used a man called William Brahman in a special way such that any germs or bacteria that came into contact with his body died instantly in the presence of doctors. Moreover, bringing together different pieces of the brain after someone was crushed by a car into pieces is one such special manifestation of supernatural power which God performed through the hands of William Brahman. Kenneth Hagin also testifies that God gave him a *special anointing* to heal the sick and went to the extent to telling him to tell the masses that God has given him that special anointing for that specific purpose. Other frontline generals who seem to have operated in the realm of *special anointing* are Kathrin Khulman, John G. Lake, Ruth Heflin, A.A Allen, John Wesley, Kenneth Hagin, Pastor Benny Hinn, Pastor Chris Oyakhilome, to mention but a few.

In our generation, special miracles whose manifestation requires a special grace from God include but are not limited to driving a car without petrol, drawing money from ATM while having a zero balance, supernatural appearance of miracle money in people's bank accounts, wallets, cars and houses; charging airtime using any randomly selected numbers, transferring the power of God into electric gargets to cause them to function, normally, charging cell phones without any connection to a charger, instantaneous disappearance of aging and wrinkles from the face of an old person, instantaneous change in one's appearance, ability to speak different languages without being taught in the natural realm, commanding rain to either fall or stop instantly, rebuking wind to stop or change direction, changing the nature of weather conditions from cold to hot vice versa, commanding clouds to envelop a place as well as walking on water or air.

3. *Creative Miracles*

In order for us to have a deeper understanding of creative miracles, let's first clarify the term "*creative*" as defined by the dictionary. This is because there is a revelation gleaned in the definition of the word that requires unveiling.

The Webster dictionary defines the word, "creative" as having the ability or power to create new things, characterised by originality, expressiveness and imaginative. As a matter of fact, when the Lord spoke through the voice of Isaiah saying, "*I'm doing a new thing! They are created now, and not so long ago, you have not heard of them before today, so you cannot say, "Yes, I knew them*" (Isaiah 48:7), He alluded to the reality of creative miracles which He is unfolding from the Throne Room in every generation. In order for you to fully grasp the revelation of creative miracles, you need to understand that God is a creator, hence there are times he does something so brand new that we don't yet have the language to describe it, nor do we have any vocabulary to speak about it. At times there isn't any vernacular, jargon or vocabulary good enough to define it. The reason why God calls it a *"new thing*" it's because it doesn't have a name as yet. It's a brand new phenomenon unfolding from the *Throne Room* of Heaven such that even the angels are still trying to comprehend it. It doesn't exist in our dictionary nor does it have a reference point hence we would need a new vocabulary to describe it. There is a rebirth of new manifestations in these end times such that humanity will not be able to look at it or recognise it because it will be completely fresh and brand new just like when *manna,* the food of angels was rained down on earth for the first time from Heaven.

A creative miracle is therefore an impartation of a completely brand new organ or body part upon an individual who previously did not have it in existence

It is a creative miracle in the very sense of the word; to create means to bring forth into manifestation or existence something that was previously not there. It is therefore a creative miracle in the sense that an organ did not exist at all in the body but now a brand new one has been imparted from Heaven. Creative miracles are products of God's glory as they are given birth to in the Glory realm, hence they are also called *creative miracles of glory.* The rationale behind creative miracles is that there is an original blue print of all human body parts resident in the *Heaven's Power House* such that in the event that someone loses one of his body parts due to either accident, misfortune or complications at conception or birth or due to any calamity or debilitating life circumstances, their parts can be instantly reinstated, imparted or restored to their original position of perfection. It should therefore be understood that in Heaven, there is a *Store House* that consists of original blue prints of all human body parts. That is why it is possible in the Glory realm for one to tap into the realm of God's power to command that specific body part to be imparted upon an individual who has a missing organ in his body. You see, God is a creator and in the capacity of sons of God, we have received an impartation of His creative ability in our spirit. In the same way God created the universe by speaking things into existence, we too can tap into the realm of God's creativity by commanding new body parts to appear in areas where they would have been lost. I'm not talking about a situation whereby God restores a body organ to its proper function but a case where God creates something that was completely not there. In a practical sense, one could command a person's left hand to shorten and be pushed back in Jesus' Name to conform to the person's original blueprint found in Heaven. For example, if God has created you to be 5 feet 10 inches, and you are slightly deformed and are only 5 feet 7 inches, then in the atmosphere of Glory, one can command your backbone to be straightened up and reach your ideal height according to the blueprint God made you to be. However, one cannot pray that you grow to be 8 feet because that is not your original blueprint in Heaven.

Prophetically speaking, taking into account the nature of this end time dispensation, God wants us to migrate or graduate from the realm of ordinary miracles to the realm of creative miracles. Did you know that creative miracles are not only performed on people's bodies but on the environment, in the atmosphere and on objects that exist in the natural realm? There is a new dimension to the realm of the miraculous in which creative miracles don't apply to living organisms only but to non-living objects as well. For instance, it might involve the appearance of new body parts of broken electric gargets such as cars, refrigerators, stoves or a visible appearance of a *star* of *glory cloud* in the atmosphere.

Quintessential examples of creative miracles include: the creation of flesh and bones where there was previously nothing, the growth and infilling of new gold teeth, appearance of hair on bold heads, supernatural appearance of miracle money in people's accounts, wallets or bags, instantaneous supernatural loss of weight as well as the appearance of eyes, hands, legs and other body parts in areas where there was completely nothing, a short person getting tall instantly as well as the instantaneous development of a pregnancy without sexual intercourse evidenced by an immediate ballooning of a tummy or giving birth to a baby within three days of pregnancy.

The Realm of signs

It is worth mentioning in a view to enhance a significant level of understanding of the dimension of *spiritual signs* that we make reference to Greek and Hebrew terminology so that we could understand this divine concept in its original context. The word sign is derived from the Greek word, *"Semeion"*, which means a sign, mark, token or symbol. Moreover, in order for us to fully grasp a deeper understanding of *spiritual signs*, we need to first understand the operation of *natural signs*. In the natural realm, a sign is something that can be seen, yet it authenticates what cannot necessarily be seen. For example, one may see a sign on the road that reads, "Johannesburg, South Africa—70 miles." A person believes the sign, which tells him that Johannesburg is 70 miles down the road. The sign points to a fact that cannot be seen. A road sign can show you to turn left, head up straight, slow down, speed humps and danger ahead. If you drive in a state of oblivion of signs, you might get into accidents. The same applies with the spiritual signs. This language is God's mother tongue, the road signs of encouragement, which unveils the way God speaks to us in a non-verbal way through coincidences, angel murmurs, thought impressions, telepathy, signs and wonders, synchronicities and other manifestations. God has been speaking to us in this symbolic language since time immemorial but in the march of progress and rise of science, technology and institutional religion, we seem to host our sense of profound mystery of divine intervention.

A sign is therefore a divine quality or spiritual manifestation whose presence or occurrence indicates the probable presence or occurrence of something else. In other words, a sign represents or points to the meaning of a divine truth that is not obvious to the natural mind as God manifest it to express a revelation. It is also a wondrous occurrence that takes place in an unusual way and transcends the common course of the natural world.

There are signs that are directed at unbelievers while there are those directed at believers. Signs given to unbelievers usually have the additional purpose of pointing them towards the truth about God and the gospel of Christ. It is an indication or evidence of something happening both in the realm of the spirit and natural, something that shows that the power of God is moving or God is at work. It always points you to a particular scenario. It always has a particular point of reference to something else. It is usually permitted by God to be brought forth or displayed so that people would believe. In Genesis 9:12, God proclaimed that,

This is the sign of the covenant which I make between me and you and every living creature that is with you for perpetual generations. I do set my rainbow in the cloud and it shall be for a sign of a convenient between me and the earth.

The rainbow in the sky is a sign, it is not a miracle. It is not a wonder but a sign because it carries a message that always points something to God's covenant of mercy after destroying the world by food. Adding another dimension to the realm of the miraculous, a sign could also be described as a manifestation or demonstration of God's supernatural power which signifies or authenticates that a person is distinguished or acknowledged. A sign is like a surety. It's like a stamp of God's approval which authenticates those He sends on specific assignments in the Kingdom. It's like a signature that God endorses when He promises something and then gives you an assurance that He will surely perform what He has promised. God uses a sign to authenticate those He sends as well as to prove that the cause that the person is defending also comes from Him. For example, if I come to you and tell you about the Holy Spirit and you don't believe, by the grace of God, I may have to give you a sign by demonstrating His power so that you may believe and be saved. Falling under the power is also a sign that something has happened in a person's spirit and also a sign that the power of God is present and someone has been touched by God. It must therefore be understood that signs are not for show-off or display purposes but for the grace of God to prevail where words alone cannot convince people of a particular divine phenomenon.

A sign also portrays or *speaks an allegoric truth* concerning the Kingdom of God. This implies that God performs signs as allegories to communicate a greater truth of the Kingdom of Heaven. For example, Jesus fed five thousand people with two loaves and five fish as a sign of His authority over limits of quantity and him being a channel of provision. He turned water into wine in a wedding at Canaan as a sign of a transition from the old religion into a new religion. He healed the blind man using mud as a sign of restoring spiritual blindness or vision of the masses. He raised Lazarus from the dead as a sign that He is the resurrection and the life and has power over death. He walked on water as a sign of authority over elements of nature. He healed the centurion's son by a spoken word as a sign of His authority over the limits of distance and space and He healed the blind man at the pool of Bethsaida as a sign to live behind the past impediments and migrate to critical kingdom matters. However, precation must be taken with regard to signs because the enemy is running a parallel display of false signs performed through false prophets in an attempt at mass deception. It is imperative that we remain aware of how the father of lies attempts to mimic signs and wonders; he will use similar performance, platforms, seasons and times but with his own purposes, contrary to the Kingdom of light.

Types of signs

Prophetic signs

Prophetic signs carry a *prophetic meaning.* Whenever they are manifested, there is always a *prophetic message* encapsulated in them. To illustrate this divine truth with quintessential examples, God showed Jeremiah a vision of a branch of almond tree and a boiling pot and then asked him a rhetoric question, "*Son of man, what do you see?*". These were prophetic signs pointing to something which God was brewing in the realm of the spirit. At times God uses physical phenomena or things in the natural to point us to a divine truth or show us what he is doing in the spirit realm. When God showed Jeremiah a boiling pot in a vision, that was a sign that danger or trouble was brewing ahead for the nation of Israel and when He showed him a branch of an almond tree, that was a sign that Israel had been disconnected or cut off from the presence of God in the same way a branch is cut off from its parent tree. God found a way of communicating to Jeremiah in the natural realm and the best was through a prophetic language of signs. Did you know that when God showed Ezekiel a valley full of dry bones, that was a *prophetic sign.* Those bones carried a prophetic meaning. It was a sign that the whole tribe of Israel was entangled in an atmosphere of mediocrity as a result of the absence of the glory of God.

To cement this divine truth with reference to scriptural evidence, the Bible talks about *the sons of Issachar who had an acute understanding of the times and seasons and knew exactly what Israel ought to do at a particular time* (1 Chronicles 12:32). But how did they know the times? Did they pray more than other tribes? No! They were simply following the Jewish calendar which showed them when to hold certain important feasts. These were prophetic signs which God used to provide prophetic direction to the whole nation of Israel. In other words, they were catapulted into the realm of *prophetic perception.* This is a spiritual sight necessary to see what God is doing in the invisible arena and in tandem with Him, you do exactly the same in the visible realm. It incorporates the ability to see the unseen, hear the unheard and then speak the unspeakable. This means that your imagination was intended by God to be the lens through which you apprehend the realms of spiritual realities. Therefore, the most integral question that we should ask ourselves in this critical season is: *In what direction is the Wind of the Spirit blowing and are we navigating the high seas of adventure by setting our sails to catch the Wind?*

Astrological signs

These are signs which are manifested in the first Heaven or galaxies when God has a message to communicate to the inhabitants of the earth. Mankind has always been fascinated with the Heavens: their beauties, their mysteries, their movements, and their surprises as David affirmed that, "*The Heavens declare the glory of God; and the firmament shows His handiwork*" (Psalm 19:1). Despite the rational, scientific understanding of most celestial happenings, such as eclipses, the glory of the galaxies can generate utter amazement. Yet, God Himself uses Heavenly phenomena as signs of momentous events. Perhaps the most famous is the "*Star of Bethlehem,"* which guided the wise men to their audience with the young King of the Jews (Matthew 2:1-2, 9-11). Do you remember the star that led the wise man to where Jesus was born in Bethlehem? That was a *sign* pointing the Kings of the earth to the Messiah.

There are also astrological signs used in Revelation involving Heavenly bodies doing the unexpected: For example, the sun darkens, the moon turns blood-red, the stars fall, and the sky itself rolls up like a scroll. Not only do these terrifying cosmic wonders signal the beginning of the Day of the Lord, but they, like the previous five seals, also serve as judgments against sinful mankind on planet Earth. Certainly, the Heavenly signs that occur in tandem with the great temblor are astounding, especially if all of them should occur within a short span of time. Joel 2:30-31 describes the same event:

> *"And I will show wonders in the heavens and in the earth: blood and fire and pillars of smoke. The sun shall be turned into darkness, and the moon into blood, before the coming of the great and terrible day of the LORD."*

In the Olivet Prophecy, Jesus repeats the warning: "*Immediately after the tribulation of those days the sun will be darkened, and the moon will not give its light; the stars will fall from heaven, and the powers of the heavens will be shaken"* (Matthew 24:29; Mark 13:24-25). Luke's rendition adds a few details: *And there will be signs in the sun, in the moon, and in the stars; and on the earth distress of nations, with perplexity, the sea and the waves roaring; men's hearts failing them from fear and the expectation of those things which are coming on the earth, for the powers of heaven will be shaken.* (Luke

21:25-26. Now, in order to fully grasp the revelation of these astrological signs, let's explain a few details. The notion of the sun being darkened may depict a solar eclipse or possibly a massive dust storm caused by a volcanic explosion on an even grander scale. Whatever the case, visibility will be severely limited, even during the daylight hours. The notion of the moon turning into blood presages calamity and death, particularly in war, as in the colour of the second horse (Revelation 6:4). The idea of stars falling in John's imagery reflects a meteor shower of immense proportions, possibly containing larger-than-normal meteorites, thus increasing the effect and making the stars themselves to fall. Because stars are a biblical symbol of angels, some theologians have suggested that this verse parallels Revelation 12:7-10, the casting out of Satan and his demons from Heaven. However, for this to have any credence, the concurrent celestial events must also be taken symbolically. The notion of the sky receding speaks of the most puzzling exposition of the earth to the wrath of God (Revelation 6:14). The apostle compares it to a scroll rolling up, or we might think of it in terms of opening a spring-loaded window blind.

End time Signs

These are the signs that point us to the second coming of the Lord Jesus Christ. In Luke 21: 7-19, Jesus informs us about the visible signs of world events which signal that the end is near. He describes the cataclysmic events in the sky and on the earth, heralding His imminent return. He reveals to us the events presaging His return in the world in Jerusalem and in the sky and earth. It is no coincidence that the first warning Jesus gives about "the sign of His coming and the end of the age" is, *"Take heed that no one deceives you"* (Matthew 24:3-4). In fact, warnings about deception are frequent throughout His Olivet Prophecy (verses 4-5, 11, 23-26, 48). The time of the end, it seems, will be one of falsehood and deceit. Secondly, the number of deceivers would be multitudinous as these frauds and agents would come in His name that is, appearing to bear His authority. In particular, the name of "Christ" would be exploited as cover for their nefarious trickery, and by this ruse, great numbers of people would be deluded. Other signs of the end of age include earthquakes, pestilences, and natural disasters which have already started unravelling in many parts of the world, heralding the imminent coming of the Lord Jesus Christ.

The Realm of wonders

It is worth exploring the divine truth that as aforementioned, a deeper understanding of the concept of wonder can be secured when we make reference to Greek and Hebrew terminology so that we could understand this divine concept in its original context. The term, *Wonder* is derived from a Greek Word, "*Teras*", meaning a prodigy, portent or something unusual that dazzles and amazes the spectator. In the context of the revelation of signs and wonders, a wonder can therefore be best described as:

A spectacular, fascinating, enthralling and hilarious spiritual experience, encounter or occurrence that causes people to be amazed. It is a feeling of surprise mingled with admiration, caused by something beautiful, unexcited, unfamiliar or inexplicable in the natural realm.

The Bible testifies that following a landslide demonstration of God's power, *fear came upon every soul as many wonders and signs were done through the apostles* (Acts 2:43). The difference between a sign and a wonder is that a sign points to something specific while a wonder appeals to the imagination, intellect and the heart of the observer and draws him to worship God. It is something that when humanity looks at, all they want to do is to ascribe unto God all the glory, honour and power due His name. This is because its occurrence defies the laws of human nature and is beyond the scope of human comprehension and reasoning.

Quintessential examples of wonders demonstrated in the Bible include: Joshua commanding the sun to go backwards and Jesus walking on water. Other examples of wonders being manifested in our generation includes the raining down of the golden glory manifested through gold dust, silver stones or supernatural oil on people's bodies, hands or on the ground during worship sessions, raining down of dew, mist and rain and angelic food from Heaven, Supernatural appearance of miracle money in people's pockets, bags and bank accounts as well as the supernatural appearance of angel feathers in people's homes or places of worship.

Wonders are also divine acts from Heaven manifested directly from the headquarters of the universe. They are possessions or properties of Heaven. In Acts 2:19, God said through the prophet Joel,

"I will show wonders in heaven above and signs in the earth beneath, blood, fire and vapour of smoke, the sun shall be turned into darkness and the moon into blood".

One major characteristic feature of wonders is that not only do they cause amazement or wonderment to the natural world but to the spirit world as well. In the spirit world you don't speak of miracles but wonders. Wonders are correspondingly to Heaven what miracles are to the earth. While miracles are only earthly occurrences, wonders transcend both realms of existence. For example, the beauty of creation, the Throne Room in Heaven, angels, spirit beings, creatures, divine substances and the glory are all wonders of Heaven.

Unlike a miracle, a wonder is not an occurrence but a phenomenon that causes those who view or experience or perceive it to just want to worship the father. The beauty of creation and Heaven is such a wonder because once you enter Heaven, you will feel like worshiping God. If an angel or a spirit being visits earth, he will not be amazed by the earth appearance or its activities but if someone from earth visits Heaven, he will definitely be amazed since the things which he sees in Heaven are a wonder to him. The angel is not amazed because the natural realm is but a shadow of things in the spirit realm, hence there is nothing new or strange about it. The man visiting Heaven will be amazed because the realm of the spirit supersedes the natural, it transcends human reasoning since you might see things which are exactly opposite to those of the natural. For example, you might see objects flying or trees playing music, things which you have never heard of in the natural realm. The reality is that some people experience miracles but then choose to keep quiet about it and continue with life as if nothing has happened but you can never see a wonder and fail to glorify God. It always leaves a permanent or non-erasable mark in the life of the beholder.

Moreover, wonders can be performed by God without the use of a human vessel. God does it all by Himself and does not need to use a man to make it happen. For example, the creation of man in the image of God is a wonder. Signs and wonders always go together and this is because unlike miracles and mighty deeds, both of them transcend both realms of existence. Their occurrence causes amazement both in the natural and spirit world. The main difference is that a sign is less in intensity of manifestation but a sign can lead to a wonder just like in (Acts 2:19), where God says, *"I will show wonders in heaven above and signs in the earth beneath"*. The highest revelation of signs and wonders is that the greatest wonder of all is Jesus. If only you could catch this revelation, then performing signs and wonders will be like taking a walk through a park.

Types of wonders

Atmospheric wonders.

Just like astrological signs, atmospheric wonders are manifested in the First Heaven. They are publicity displayed in the galaxies and expressed by the language of starts, moon and the sky. Let me substantiate this divine truth with reference to a quintessential scripture in Psalm 19:1-4:

"The Heavens declare the glory of God and the stars proclaim the work of His hands; day to day, they pour forth speech, and night reveals knowledge. There is no speech, nor are there words where their voice is not heard. Their line has gone out through all the earth, and their utterances to the end of the world."

A hermeneutical analysis of this scripture unveils the divine truth that the glory of God is also resident and unreservedly manifested through galaxies. This is the glory of the *First Heaven*. In fact, that's the key to everything that exists. Everything God ever created was designed with a purpose of subscribing to Him, all the glory. That is why the Bible says the Heavens declare the glory of God. Do you notice that in our above opening scripture, the Bible says the stars have a speech and a voice? How is that possible? It's because sound waves are embedded in everything that exists on earth, including stars, rocks, food, trees and everything ever created. Do you know that speech was one of the first ingredients that created everything else you see and the invisible things you don't see? Therefore, the idea of stars giving a speech alludes to the spiritual reality that sounds waves can be transmitted through speech from both living and non-living objects. This is the essence of atmospheric wonders. They always leave you with an appetite that yearns to worship God.

The greater truth is that when God made the inanimate creation, when He made the Heavens and the Earth, they were for His glory and this is an incontestable reality in both the spirit realm and the natural realm. Even those who are least inclined to study the Heavens must at times have been stunned by the beauty of a spectacular sunset, especially if we are looking out to the sea beyond a quiet coastline. Even without articulate sounds, and words, the Heavens eloquently declare the glory of God. Graphically speaking, a work of art is the glory of the artist who created it because it's something which brings glory to him. In his work, the artist expresses himself and the artistic masterpiece honours the artist's skills. By the same token, the whole creation is a work of art which glorifies God, demonstrating His wisdom and power.

Natural wonders

These are a product of nature; the beauty and majesty of God expressed through natural phenomenon. The greater truth is that unknown to many people, nature exhibits His glory. His glory is revealed to man's mind through the material world in many ways, and often in different ways to different people. Do you remember when God rained down manna the food of angels down to earth for the children of Israel to eat in the wilderness? That was a wonder of God manifested in the natural realm. This is akin to the falling of gold dust, diamonds and precious stones coupled with miracle money which is becoming a common phenomenon in the Body of Christ during worship sessions in the current times. It is of paramount importance to highlight right from the onset the divine truth that contrary to what multitudes of believers presume, the manifestation of *gold dust* and other precious stones is not a new phenomenon in the realm of God. Taking centre stage recently in packed churches is a new phenomenon that really is not that new. It is the appearance of "*gold dust*" and the transformation of fillings or crowns into "*gold.*" These transformations have been hailed as a new move of God that is sweeping the charismatic churches worldwide. Throughout ages, the wealth of Heaven and God's supernatural provision has been manifested in divergent ways, whether it be, gold dust, gold fakes or gold teeth. However, the gravity and intensity of its manifestation is heightened in these last days in what I call *"a new wave of gold manifestations"*.

The truth of the matter is that the unparalleled degree of manifestation of gold dust in this end time season is not intended to be just a *Church phenomenon*, but a *Church revelation.* The Bible foretold that signs and wonders of such a great magnitude would be seen in the last days, and the manifestation of gold dust, diamonds, silver as well as other precious stones is one of them. Over the last few years, there has been a lot of reports of gold and silver dust appearing upon people, mainly in charismatic Christian meetings. Some have also received gold coins, gems, as well as oil dripping from hands of individuals in their homes and yards. Others are receiving angelic manifestations seen above them as flowing beautiful transparent figures and circles of faint light referred to as *angel orbs.* Moreover, angels' feathers, gemstones, coloured sparkle and gold dust are accelerating. Many are attaching prophetic significance to this current wave of gold manifestations, heralding a new phase in the church, being prophetic of the establishment of God's Kingdom on earth, or being symbolic of the transference of wealth from the wicked into the Church. Angels of precious stones who work in conjunction with angels of prosperity shall be seen on the rise, dominating the scene where God is worshiped in truth and in spirit.

To cement the revelation of this divine phenomenon with reference to practical evidence, manifestations of *gold dust"* on hands and other parts of the body has been reported occasionally in some meetings. These are what appears to be tiny specks of gold appearing in the hands, where wiping the hands has the effect of depositing the gold specks on clothing. This manifestation appears to be transferrable, either by prayer or by simple contact, others do exhibit this manifestation. The *law of contagious experience* seem to have taken its course in this new move of God. For example, during one of our meetings, gold dust started appearing in the hands of one lady. Upon wiping her hands on her clothing, the gold dust appeared to have been deposited upon her clothing and yet the amount of the dust on her hands seem to remain constant as if the gold dust spontaneously reappeared after wiping on clothing. This woman then started laying her hands on anyone around her lining up to receive the blessing and many others reported the appearance of gold dust on their own hands.

Moreover, Gold dust was reportedly appearing not only in hands, but also on the face and in the hair of the congregants. There were even reports of *gold fakes* appearing in the pages of people's bibles, cars, bags and houses. Not only gold, but manifestations of silver and even diamonds and other precious stones such as onyx, pearl, jasper and emerald has also been reported. Others found the gold dust in the prayer rooms and on worship instruments and it was constantly appearing further and further back along the walls until it finally met at the back doors of the sanctuary. Moreover, people reported gold appearing spontaneously in their teeth. In some cases, the dark amalgam fillings in the teeth appears to have transmuted itself into gold fillings. In other cases, gold in the shape of crosses appeared in teeth, and also gold crowns covering the teeth. Along with the "*gold teeth*"manifestations, occurrences of gold dust, gold fakes are increasing worldwide. Shiny sparkles of diamond dust and silver dust were received during services as people received the gold inlays and silver fillings, some in the form of a cross and the actuality of gemstones falling from the atmosphere, inside churches. Accompanying this divine manifestation, it has been further reported that a "*Glory Cloud*" appeared during worship services. In short, a cloud of gold-like dust was hovering up by the roof. It caused some hysteria during worship as multitudes of people were crowding together in exhilaration and gathering underneath it. These are some of the enthralling natural wonders which God is precipitating upon the Body of Christ in this very hour so that the masses can believe in Him.

Throne Room wonders

These pertain to wonders that take place at the Throne Room in Heaven. Such wonders is what Paul described as *something inexpressible for man to tell,* following his visitation to the Throne Room. Inexpressible in the sense that it's a wonder, it produces amazement in a way that cannot be described by the human vocabulary. In the Spiritual World, the only light that lights up the entire universe is the light of Christ that shines from His throne. This light does not cast any shadows but rather flows right through all living creatures in the spiritual realm. Even the light of the brightest angels is the refraction of the light of Christ. Those who are on the earth spheres do not see the light of Christ all the time because in the spiritual world, you need the same equivalent spiritual level to see in that same level of spiritual light. From time to time, the light of Christ would shine according to the needs of individuals in the earth sphere but the visibility of that glorious light has to be diminished according to the level of the individual. However, the presence of Christ is always there without the individual spirit, who is not developed to the higher glory, realising it. This light is also the very means by which all life in every sphere is sustained and nourished. The light of the spiritual world is different from the physical sunlight that the material earth has. It is interpenetrating and shines through the physical realm. Therefore, when we look at a human being from the spiritual realm, we do not really see the physical body, it appears like a mist or envelope – although this also depends on the spiritual development of the spirit; those who are still earth-bound see the material realm as a solid substance. The well-developed spirits of the higher spirit realm see right into the spirit and soul of humans.

There are many "*Heavens*" where the presence of God is manifested to a different degree in each sphere. All planetary spheres of God have their own Heaven and progress to the Heaven of Heavens where God dwells. The glory of each Heaven is progressively greater with the least glory in the sphere of Heaven nearer the earth and the greatest glory in the sphere of Heaven nearest to the Heaven of Heavens. Although there are innumerable Heavens in each creation of God, all the Heavens and creations can be classified into three main categories: the First Heaven containing planetary spheres that belong to the particular solar systems, the Second Heaven containing the celestial spheres which belong to the space between solar systems, and the Third Heaven containing the God-spheres which radiate directly outwards from the Throne of God Himself. The progression of spiritual growth is not just in glory alone but also in dimension until it reaches the dimension of God where all dimensions known to us of time, space, omnipresence, and so forth disappear because God is outside of all the dimensions which He has created. For a human spirit that has just left the mortal body, even the first sphere of light would be a paradise compared to the present physical world. There is no death or decay or any of the earthly imperfections; only love, peace and joy.

God is able to manifest Himself in any part of the Spiritual Universe without leaving His throne. This manifestation takes a spiritual form with all the glory of God as tailored to the specific glory realm of the place where the revelation of God is unfolded. Angels and spirits in the highest spheres also possess a measure of this ability to project their presence in a spiritual form without leaving their places of abode. This spiritual form is alive with the life of the spirit and responsive to all the thoughts, will and emotion of the originating source. There is no natural comparison to this. Time, space and reality in the spiritual world are not as unbending as their physical counterparts (of time, space and matter). Part of the progress in the Spiritual World is to break free from always thinking in our physical three dimensional ways. For a deeper revelation of the wonders of Heaven, I would kindly refer you to one of my anointed books titled, *"The Divine revelation of The Realm of The Spirit"*.

The Realm of mighty deeds

A mighty deed is what I would colloquially describe as *the extreme end of scale.* It's the manifestation of God's power to its extreme degree in the natural realm. When the gravity, intensity and degree of supernatural manifestation is so aggravated, deep-seated, far-reaching or heightened such that it even confounds the subjects in both the natural and spirit realm, it is said to be a mighty deed. What makes an act to qualify to be a mighty deed is the depth of spiritual experience or degree of manifestation. Some experiences are so deep such that they have a profound supernatural effect on the bodies of those who see or experience them. When we talk about mighty deeds, we are not just talking about divine acts performed by man under the direction of the anointing or using their faith. Instead, we are talking about a scenario in which God takes up residence in a body of a man to perform mighty acts that transcends human comprehension. Mighty deeds are usually performed in the glory realm of when the glory of God is manifested in a specific territory in the natural realm. In most cases God does it alone without the help of human vessels. This is the reason why when the glory of God is manifested to a heightened degree, the dead rises up on their own accord even without anybody praying for them.

A mighty deed is a manifestation of the supernatural power of God in extreme cases and radical situations where human comprehension and reasoning cannot suffice.

It is the fullness of God's supernatural strength and mighty power displayed or revealed to man and its manifestation is so remarkable, tremendous and overwhelming to such an extent that it leaves a non-erasable mark, an unforgettable experience and a permanent legacy in a generation. For example the raising of a man from the dead as a result of contact with the bones of Elijah four hundred years after his death is an undeniably a mighty deed. Even though believers are still preaching about it, many still find it hard to fully comprehend how that came about. Its impact or mark in the history of humanity has such far reaching spiritual consequences and repercussions that can be felt across many generations after its occurrence. Therefore, it has a profound eternal effect and can transcend both realms of existence. Another quintessential example of a mighty deed is the resurrection of the Lord Jesus Christ Himself from the dead. It's a mighty deed in that no one in the whole universe, Heaven included could have undertaken such a task, except the Lord Jesus Christ Himself. It is therefore a distinguished, clear cut occurrence far beyond the level of ordinary miracles. A mighty deed could also be described as the fullness of God's power manifested or exhibited through the hand of a man to accomplish His work. For example, Acts 6:1 affirms that *the signs of an apostle were wrought amongst you in miracles, signs and wonders and mighty deeds.* What determines an occurrence whether it is a mighty deed or not is the degree or intensity of its manifestation. They are called mighty deeds because they are mighty in God to the pulling down of strongholds of religion, humanism, atheism, philosophy, psychology and every sphere of human and spiritual endeavour.

Due to the sacred nature of mighty deeds, God gives apostles and prophets the grace to undertake them. Despite the fact that God has an open door grace policy and can use anybody to accomplish ministerial tasks, not everybody can move in the dimension of mighty deeds. These require an extreme measure of grace and calling for one to do them. I have heard of a man whose head was crashed by a car into pieces to the extent that his brains were unceremoniously scattered on the floor and William Braham came and commanded the pieces of brain to join up together into the man's body and his life came back. Smith Wigglesworth also caught a revelation that the dead can be raised and God used him mightily in that area to the extent that he would drag a dead body out of a coffin and then command it to walk. He was more than convinced that no one should die before his time, hence he permitted no one in his locality to depart without his permission. All these are quintessential examples of mighty deeds performed in the natural world. And this is the dimension into which God is elevating believers in this end time season. All the acts of resurrection performed by saints like Saint Patrick, Saint Denis, Saint and Francis Xavier which I described earlier in this book were phenomenal mighty deeds. Raising someone from the dead after spending 6 weeks in the grave or when the body is already rotting and in some cases when its bones and skeleton only is definitely a mighty deed. It's something that even angels are still trying to comprehend or look into.

These are mighty in God to the extent that even the spirit realm acknowledges their occurrence. For example, if one is raised from the dead, even in the spirit realm it is a mighty dead because in the spirit, things do not die, so when something is raised from the dead in the natural, realm, it transcends even the spirit world. That is why the resurrection of Jesus Christ from the dead is held in high esteem both in the spirit world and natural world because it is an occurrence that does not take place in the spirit world. Have you also not heard of how following the resurrection of Jesus Christ thousands of saints who had died in the Lord were raised from the dead and ripped their graves apart such that they were seen walking in the streets of Jerusalem in broad day light? That was a mighty deed that caused a shaking both in the natural world and spirit world. Imagine the headlines of that morning saying, "*Thousands of saints raised from the dead and seen walking in the streets of Jerusalem!*". That was a spectacle – phenomenal, remarkable and enthralling. Wonders are performed by God without the use of a human vessel. God does it all by Himself and does not need to use a man to make it happen. For example, even man in his creation in the image of God is a wonder but in the case of mighty deeds, the act is performed by God through a man. That is why God uses apostles and prophets because these are the ones given the highest level of grace to use God's power to transcend the natural realm. For example, God does not need a man to create the Heavens but he needs a man to raise another man from the dead. In this context, the resurrection or raising the dead is categorised in the Fourth dimension of the realm of the miraculous as a mighty deed. This is because of its degree of intensity in manifestation. *Rapture* is one of those experiences that can be categorised as a mighty deed. To have believers raptured at the same time all around the world I believe is an act that is going to shake not only the whole world but the spirit world as well.

CHAPTER SIX

THE SIXTH DIMENSION:

THE DIMENSION OF GLORY

In its original context, the Greek word for glory is *doxa,* which means brilliance, splendour, brightness, glittering appearance, radiance, flamboyance, magnificence, excellence or pre-eminence. The Hebrew word for glory is *kabowd*, which means honour, dignity, abundance, majesty, admiration, tribute, heavy, weighty or rich. By definition, the glory is a tangible and visible supernatural manifestation of the fullness or totality of God from the realm of the spirit into the realm of the physical. This implies that the glory is God in His totality or state of perfection and completeness. It is the intrinsic essence of who God is characterised or manifested by His nature, character, being, attributes or virtues. This implies that the glory is the nature of God and an exact representation or extension of his being. It proceeds from him; it is part of His being. It could also be described as the divine impartation and revelation of the substance, heaviness, imminence, supremacy of the transcending presence of God in the affairs of humanity. This implies that the glory is the impartation of the nature and the life of God upon a human vessel. Moreover, it is the highest dimension, depth, realm or level of concentration of God's supreme power or sovereignty manifested in the realm of the physical, which transcends all natural laws, principles and processes.

Contextually, the glory is the source of all manifestations. The power, anointing and mantle come as a result of His glory. The glory is what brings the presence because the presence is a radiation or refection of His glory. Philosophically speaking, the presence is what brings the anointing because the anointing is an impartation of His ability when He rests upon a vessel. The anointing is what brings about the power because power is an end product that comes when one is anointed. The glory is the source, then anointing is an intermediate product and power is an end product. Paul unveiled the highest revelation of Christianity in the New Testament when he declared in 2 Corinthians 4:6, *Christ is the glory of God* and we know that Christ is also the Word of God since the scripture says in the beginning was the *Word,* the *Word* was God and the *Word* was with God. This implies that if Christ is the glory of God, who is also the word of God, that means the word of God is the glory of God. Hence, the phrase *"In the beginning was the Word, the Word was God and the Word was with God"* can be interpreted or re-written as *"In the beginning was the Glory, the Glory was God and the Glory was with God."* This leads us to an inevitable conclusion that the word of God is the glory of God. By the same token, it suffices to conclude that the small voice that spoke to Elijah after all the manifestation had taken place was God's glory. It was not His power, it was not His presence, it was not His anointing, but it was His *glory.* It represented His very being, His nature and originality. The small still voice came from His being, it proceeded from the father, hence that voice was His glory.

It is of paramount significance to highlight at this stage that each one of us carries a measure of God's glory and presence. If that glory is increased in our life, we are more enabled to move in higher realms of power. We all receive proportional measure of glory but our zeal, level of expectation, hunger for more is what distinguishes us from the rest. Just like Moses, although he had known God just for a short time period, he came to a stage whereby he asked God show him His glory. And when God showed him His glory there was a difference in the relationship of God in his life. It is a greater truth that God relates to you at the point of glory. And it's important for us to seek after the glory and the presence of God in our life. All of us know what God's presence is. But we need to hunger even more for God's glory. We need to desire for more of His glory because it is through His glory that the anointing, presence and power comes.

What makes the glory so spectacular as compared to other spiritual substances is that when one departs for Heaven, he doesn't leave with the anointing and the mantle but with the Glory. The anointing and mantle remains on earth to fall upon the next generation but the glory goes with the person to Heaven. This is because it is the level of glory that would determine in which realm or plane of Glory the person will live in Heaven. In actual fact, the anointing was never given to Heaven but it is given to earthly vessels to operate. This is why Elisha did not go with his anointing and mantle to Heaven such that even after more than four hundred years, his bones still retained the anointing. In Heaven you don't go with the anointing, power or presence but you go with the glory because it is the glory upon you that will determine the realm of heavenly glory for you to be placed in Heaven. Spiritually speaking, the glory is the only spiritual substance that is permitted to enter Heaven. Hence, in this end time dispensation, there is a progressive *transition from the anointing the glory of God.* The truth of the matter is that many people know the anointing but they don't know the glory. This is because the anointing has been so much advertised and publicised in the church but very view believers have been able to fully tap into the realm of glory.

There are spiritual truths that we need to put into correct perspective. In the realm of God, there are greater truths and lesser truths. We can receive the anointing, the mantle or the presence but what makes the glory so special and sacred is that we don't receive it but we walk into it. The word of God says in Colossians 1:27, that *Christ in you, the Hope of glory.* This implies that the glory of God is already resident in your spirit in measures and degrees. Our duty is to draw from within us by yielding more to God and praying in the Holy Ghost and power will flow. This revelation comes out clear when we cross reference to another scripture in John 7:38 that *out of your belly shall flow rivers of living waters.* While this scripture could be interpreted to mean the anointing, it actually refers to the glory because it is the Glory that is resident in your spirit and flows out as power is displayed, hence when we move in the power of God we actually exhibit and display that glory that comes from within us.

A DIVINE REVELATION OF THE DIMENSION OF THE ANOINTING AND GLORY

It is worth exploring the truth that while the anointing is given to an individual for service to complete specific tasks, the glory is given for elevation or promotion in the spirit. The glory comes as a result of one having completed successfully the delegated divine tasks. Hence, the anointing is what breeds the glory because the anointing causes one to execute tasks and brings them to perfect completion which would then entitle one to be in a position to receive the glory. In other words, the anointing lays a fertile ground for the glory of God to be revealed.

It is a greater truth that the anointing is given to bring the glory of God into manifestation. This is the ultimate purpose of the anointing in the kingdom. You get to see the glory of God through the anointing because the anointing is what connects you to the glory of God .It lays a groundwork or preparation platform for the glory to be revealed or manifested. God's presence and power are resident in the anointing, hence any man of God who taps into the realm of the anointing and manifests miracles, signs and wonders ushers the glory of God on the scene. In this case, the anointing reveals or manifests the glory of God. In Acts:10:38, the Bible speaks of *how God anointed Jesus of Nazareth with the Holy Ghost and with power: who went about doing good, and healing all that were oppressed of the devil, for God was with Him.* This implies that the anointing is what certifies, establishes and authenticates God's unwavering supremacy, divine plans and purpose in the light of His creation. In the absence of the anointing, the glory is not revealed. Some people think that the anointing and the glory is one and the same thing. On the other extreme some are just so obsessed about the anointing and in the process neglects the glory that brings that anointing. That is why in this end time dispensation there is an emphasis in the supernatural for a progressive transition from the realm of the anointing to the realm of God's glory and this is what forms the theme of the end time message. The anointing is like the light. The light is what manifests the glory of the sun. Without the sun, there is no light and by the same token without the glory, there is no anointing. But it is the light which makes manifest the glory of the sun. In the same manner, it is the anointing that manifests the glory of God.

However, elevation into higher realms of the anointing is largely dependent on the persistent and progressive application of spiritual laws and principles while migration into higher realms of glory is dependent on the will of God. Moreover, the anointing operates by human discretion, prerogative or initiative while the glory works by divine initiative. You operate by faith in the realm of the anointing but in the realm of glory, you operate by God's initiative and divine sovereignty since it is an unknown dimension. However, only if the glory does not manifest, can you tap into the realm of gifts, faith and the anointing. When operating in the realm of glory, God demands a greater degree of humility and dependence on Him. This is because elevation into higher realms of glory demands pure motives and boldness in the spirit. The anointing is the ability given to man by God to do whatever He has called him to do but the glory is God doing His work and operating according to His sovereignty and initiative. It is therefore stricter to operate in the glory than in the anointing. Mistakes for operating in the anointing can be overlooked but God demands accountability and judgement for any misconduct exhibited in the display of glory. It is much quicker to accomplish tasks under the glory than with the anointing. In Luke 5:1-11, after spending a night fishing without any success, Peter received an instruction from Jesus to cast the nets into the deep and instantaneously, he caught a multitude of fish within a split of a moment. This is because when the glory of God manifests, everything accelerates. Millions of souls can be reached within a short period of time when operating under the glory. As a matter of fact, divine tasks which could have taken years to complete are completed within a moment. Just like when 3000 people were converted to Christ in one day because of the glory (Acts 2:41). On the basis of the scripture, it is therefore evident that the realm of glory is a higher dimension that operates on different spiritual laws and principles as compared to that of the anointing. Therefore, a man knows he is in the dimension of glory when he does not operate in his personal measure of faith and the anointing. When one operates in the anointing, there is a tendency to feel physically exhausted because people place a demand on the anointing. However, operating in the glory produces more strength and power.

The anointing is a substitute substance for the glory. You can substitute the glory for the anointing but you can never substitute the anointing for the glory because the operation of the glory is not under human control. You operate under the anointing only when the glory of God does not show up but when it does, you give way to God's presence. While the anointing is temporary as comes and take off depending on the nature of service, the glory takes a permanent abode or spiritual residence in humanity and begins to attract favour, blessings, promotion, divine health and prosperity in the life of a person. That is why Paul affirms in Philippians 4:19 that *the Lord supplies all our needs according to the riches in Christ glory*. That means all our needs, demands, prosperity, increase is regulated by the pre-eminence of glory. The glory is therefore the ultimate key to every prosperity, success, promotion and increase. It is a prerequisite for all dimensions of prosperity. Hence, there is such a thing called *Prosperity by the glory*.

The anointing and faith are governed by spiritual laws and principles but there is no law that governs the glory. For example, we have the law of faith and the law of the anointing that prescribes specific principles to be followed or applied for these to manifest but there is no such thing as the law of glory. The glory is not governed by any law since it is administered directly by God himself. God created the laws for the universe and not for himself hence He is not accountable to any law. He did not create the law for himself but for the universe hence his glory transcends all his laws. Operating in the dimension of glory therefore guarantees one success, greater power and greater manifestations.

TRANSITION FROM THE REALM OF THE ANOINTING TO THE REALM OF GLORY

It is a typical scenario across a broad spectrum of Christian faith that many believers have had spiritual encounters and experiences in the anointing but a few have experienced the tangibility of God' glory. Due to reasons attributable to a lack of revelation, in some instances, many Biblical teachings in the church are centred on matters of faith, gifting and the anointing, at the expense of the glory. The consequence of this divine phenomenon is that there is so much emphasis placed on faith and the anointing and less on the glory. This is a gross representation of spiritual truths taking into account the reality that the Body of Christ is living on the edge as we have been ushered right into the very special moments of glory in the calendar of God.

However, it suffices to highlight that in this end time dispensation there is an alarming outcry and emphasis in *the supernatural for a progressive transition from the realm of the anointing to the realm of God's glory*. There is a paradigm shift and global migration from the substance of the anointing into the transcending higher realms of Glory. In essence, there is a drastic and profound transformation in the governance and administration of the anointing to the release of the glory in unfathomable ways never imagined before. While in the past decades there has been an emphasis for a transition from the realm of senses into the realm of faith and from the realm of faith into the realm of the anointing; now Heavens demands a further migration into higher realms of glory. This is a major characteristic feature of the end time dispensation which shall see the masses being catapulted into higher realms of glory to experience what they have never seen, heard, conceived or experienced before. In an endeavour to awaken this present generation to the reality of permanently moving, operating and functioning in the revelation of glory, God is raising a unique breed of ministers who shall actively drive, spearhead, rigorously participate or partake in the final move of God's glory and He is leading them on the path of transition from the anointing into the glory so that they can enter into the river of God's Shekinah.

It is therefore a greater truth that with faith and the gifts of the spirit, we can reach individuals and with the anointing we can reach the multitudes but with the glory we can reach the whole world in a spilt of a moment .The realm of glory is a higher dimension beyond the realm of gifts and the anointing, hence we need to tap into the realm of glory for a global manifestation. This dispensation therefore marks the beginning of the season of divine exploration and discovery to discover things in the supernatural that have never experienced before. Increased visitations to the Throne Room shall therefore become a common experience as people are launched into the depths of God's presence to explore and unleash the fullness of His glory. The opening of the Heavens to connect man with the release of the rain of glory shall consequentially result in many being elevated to greater heights in the supernatural. In terms of efficiency, frequency and impact, this transition from anointing to glory is like a person who moves from driving a car into driving an aeroplane. While both a car and a plane are means of transportation but the frequency, efficiency and speed with which they operate is totally different. By the same token while both the anointing and glory are aspects of God's power, the frequency of the glory, the level, depth, dimension and area of operation is much higher and greater as compared to the anointing. This revelation must propel your faith to move and tap into higher realms of awaiting glory. A car would stop at the robots, be intercepted by the road blocks at times be hindered or delayed by the speed of other cars on the road. On the contrary to the anointing, the glory cannot be stopped, does not operate on spiritual laws, cannot be hindered or delayed since it is the highest concentration of God's power.

TRANSITION FROM THE REALM OF THE ANOINTING TO THE REALM OF GLORY

THE SECRET TO TAPING INTO HIGHER REALMS OF GLORY

A migration into any dimension or realm in the supernatural is always governed by the revelation and a change in the application of spiritual laws and principles. In view of the above, it is of paramount importance to highlight the fact that any migration or elevation from one level of the anointing to the other requires paying a price through undertaking intense sacrifices and strenuous spiritual exercises such as intense meditation on the word of God, persistent fasting as well as relentless prayer and practising the presence. And it happens that after advancing through various levels and dimensions of the anointing in the supernatural, one reaches a *breakthrough or ceiling point* beyond which he can no longer proceed further under reasonable circumstances. This is what I call the *Limitation of the Anointing*. When this happens, this serves as an indication of one's readiness to make a transition from the anointing to the realm of glory.

Firstly, when one has reached a level of faith in the anointing in which nothing new is happening, then this is an indication that one is ready to enter the dimension of glory. It is recorded in Luke 5:1-11 that, after Peter had spent the whole night fishing and without catching anything, but when Jesus stepped on the scene and ushered the glory of God and commanded him to cast into the deep, Peter was convinced that it was time to change his career from that of fishing fish to that of fishing souls. You also require the right timing to migrate into higher realms of Glory. You might have been labouring hard or migrating from one church to the other pursuing man of God or seeking after the anointing but when it's time to migrate to a higher realm of glory, Jesus will show upon on the scenes.

Secondly, contrary to the reality that a transition from one level of the anointing to the other requires undertaking certain spiritual exercises, transition into the realm of glory requires revelation knowledge for one cannot move into what has not been revealed to him. Without revelation, we can never see beyond the natural senses. The key that grants us access to the manifestation of glory in the natural realm is revelation since it can trigger or provoke a supernatural experience. The level of revelation one has is directly proportional to the dimension of Glory one can be elevated into. God's glory must be revealed by the Spirit, it cannot be discovered by research or understood by reason. That is the reason why the church has been for long seeking the manifestation of glory without any success because they lacked the required revelation knowledge to manifest that glory. Hence, for the glory of God to manifest, it must be captured, received and recognised by our spirits through the revelation of the spirit.

Thirdly, a perennial hunger, unquencheable thirst and an insatiable appetite for the new revelation of God's glory is also another indication to portray the church's readiness to migrate into higher realms of glory. A desire and hunger for the supernatural and to function in the heightened realm of the supernatural in signs and wonders is another indication that one is ready to enter the realm of glory. Fourthly, Spiritual readiness or preparedness is another pre-requisite to moving into higher realms of glory. Whenever the glory of God shows up, it brings forth new spiritual encounters and experiences, unusual manifestations, creative miracles, signs and wonders, some of which might be peculiar or complex to understand. We must therefore be ready to deal with any manifestation lest we grieve the spirit. There must not be any mistakes for operating in the glory to avoid side effects like Uzzah who mistakenly touched the ark of God and died (2 Samuel 6: 7).

Fifthly, it is the openness and willingness for the graduation and progressive migration from one level of faith to the other, from one level of anointing to another and from one level of glory to another that will catapult one to higher realms of glory. Lack of momentum can restrict or limit a man from operating in the realm of glory. Moreover, the dimension of glory requires a complete dependence on God. Anyone who is not willing to submit under the supremacy or pre-eminence or sovereignty of God is not ready for the realm of glory. One has to make an effort to align his attitude, character and mentality to the will of God. Moreover, it is bad theology humanism and carnality that will prevent one from reaching higher dimensions of glory. Lastly, a progressive and exhaustive migration through the seven realms of the depths of the supernatural such as realm of trances, realm of open vision, realm of transportation, angelic realm, realm of visitation and realm of translation could also serve as an acid test and evidence that one is ready for the dimension of glory. Successfully rising up the ladder across the seven dimensions of the universe is also evidence that one is ready for the dimension of glory. The ability to pay a greater price to see the manifestation of Glory is therefore incontestable evidence that indicates one's readiness for higher realms of glory (Psalms 63:1-2).

A Divine Revelation of the Distinction between the Dimension of the Anointing and the Dimension Glory

It is a fact that in the current scenario across a broad spectrum of Christian faith, multitudes of believers are familiar with the manifestation of the anointing but know little about the manifestation of the glory. This is because in the recent times, more emphasis has been placed on believers walking in the anointing as opposed to the glory hence, few of them have managed to tap into the realm of God's glory. The consequence or result of this trend has been the spiritual production of believers who are full of the substance of the anointing but devoid of the glory which sustains that anointing. Therefore, we should learn to move in the realm of God's glory just as we learn to move in the anointing. We should learn to develop in glory as we develop in the anointing. Contrary to what multitudes of Christians across a broad spectrum of Christian faith presume, having an anointing is not as same thing as moving in God's glory, which alludes to His attributes. The anointing is a part of God, operating through us. Basically, the anointing of God is a manifestation of the power of God while the glory of God is a manifestation of His attributes. It is only one aspect of His power because there are many divergent aspects of God's power. In view of the above, carefully consider the following divine truth:

Holistically speaking, God's power demonstrated in the arena of spiritual warfare is called MIGHT, God's power manifested in the arena of finances is called WEALTH, God's power demonstrated in the arena of territorial governance is called is DOMINION, God's power manifested in the arena of ministry is called the ANOINTING, but God's power demonstrated in the arena of sovereignty is called THE GLORY, which is the highest dimension of power in the realm of God.

The anointing of God is the tangible manifestation of God's power while the glory of God is the manifestation of God's person and attributes. Both are manifestations. Both are touchable. Both have degrees or levels of manifestation. Both are of a heavenly materiality. Both are manifested together inseparably, just as God's attributes and power are inseparable parts of His being. The manifestation of the anointing of God is in direct proportion to the manifestation of the glory of God. Although the anointing and the glory can be attributable or traced to the same source, the glory supersedes the anointing in divergent spheres. The following are therefore aspects of distinction between operating in the anointing and operating in the glory:

It is of paramount significance to unveil right from the onset the divine truth that in the context of this revelation, there are two ways through which God administers His power on earth, which is through qualified agent *(anointing)* or by Himself *(glory)*. No matter the various ways God has shown His power, they can be summed up in two categorical words, that is the *anointing* (manifestation), and the *glory* (revelation). These two stages equate to direct versus indirect engagement or involvement of the person of God, which ushers in His power. The application of the power of God is designed to achieve or materialize God's purpose. Whether channelled through alternative source or direct application, the result must be the same. Remember that the person of the Godhead must be involved to experience the power of God. The power of God cannot be imitated or manufactured because it is part of God's special personal qualities and qualifications.

You get to see the glory of God through the anointing because the anointing is what connects you to the glory of God.

It is worth exploring the divine truth that the anointing lays a groundwork or preparation platform for the glory to be revealed or manifested. God's presence and power are resident in the anointing, hence any man of God who taps into the realm of the anointing and manifests miracles, signs and wonders, ushers the glory of God on the scene. In this case, the anointing reveals or manifests the glory of God. In Acts 10:38, the Bible speaks of *how God anointed Jesus of Nazareth with the Holy Ghost and with power, who went about doing good, and healing all those oppressed of the devil, for God was with Him.* In other words, what qualified Him to usher such an immeasurable glory of God manifested through signs and wonders is the anointing. This implies that the anointing is what certifies and authenticates God's unwavering supremacy, divine plans and purpose in the light of His creation. In the absence of the anointing, the glory is not revealed because the anointing is what prepares us for the glory. Faith calls the anointing and the anointing calls the glory but both are key dimensions of the supernatural.

It is a typical scenario in some charismatic cycles that some people presume that the anointing and the glory is one and the same thing hence they are devoid of revelation knowledge to press from the realm of the anointing into that of glory. On the other extreme, some are just so obsessed about the anointing and in the process neglects the glory that brings that anointing. That is why in this end time dispensation there is an emphasis in the supernatural for a progressive transition from the realm of the anointing to the realm of God's glory and this is what forms the central theme and agenda of Heaven in these current times. Philosophically speaking, the anointing is like the light. The light is what manifests the glory of the sun. Without the sun, there is no light and by the same token without the glory, there is no anointing. However, it is the light which makes manifest the glory of the sun and in a similar vein, it is the anointing that manifest the glory of God.

It is worth mentioning that elevation into higher realms of the anointing is largely dependent on the persistent and progressive application of spiritual laws and principles while migration into higher realms of glory is dependent on the sovereign will of God.

The anointing operates by human discretion, prerogative or initiative while the glory works by divine initiative

This implies that you operate by faith in the realm of the anointing but in the realm of glory, you operate by God's initiative and divine sovereignty since it is an unknown dimension. However, only if the glory does not manifest, can you tap into the realm of gifts, faith and the anointing. When operating in the realm of glory, God demands a greater degree of humility and dependence on Him. This is because elevation into higher realms of glory demands pure motives and boldness in the spirit.

We operate in the anointing to make things happen but in the realm of glory, everything has already happened.

It is worth exploring the truth that when you operate in the glory realm, it's not necessarily the level of faith that brings about a miracle when your faith brings you to the realm where things have already happened. It is not your faith that is trying to make something happen because you are in a realm where it already exists. Therefore, when operating in the realm of glory, don't allow your mind to be programmed to think according to earthly time because you have dominion over time. Heavens are perfect, there is nothing you lack or need, while the earth is in a prophetic drama, Heaven is a realm where it has already happened. It is not going to happen. It has already happened, yet in the earth it has not happened yet. To shade clarity and more light on this revelation, it is of paramount importance to highlight the divine truth that there are two dimensions of time, the *earthly time* measured in hours and seconds and *eternity or Heaven's time* which is infinite. But the truth is that God operates according to the eternal time which falls outside our time dimension in the natural realm and has given us the ability to have dominion over time in the natural realm by superimposing eternal time on the earthly time. So, with regard to possessing your possessions, you have to decide whether you are going to wait for the earthly time for them to mature so that you can possess them or you are going to shift to the eternal realm, which is Heavens' time to possess your blessings before time.

The greater truth is that while modern day believers are so much conscious about the issue of timing, you need to understand that when operating in the glory realm, things happen before the time they are scheduled to happen. Do you know that when Jesus changed water into wine at a wedding in Galilee, that miracle happened before its time? Why do I say so? Because even Jesus said it himself that, "*Woman why do you bother me before My time?*" The miracle was not supposed to happen at that time but it happened because Mary placed a demand on the anointing upon Jesus, thereby provoking Him to usher in the miracle before its time. That is the same principle by which Jesus ushered an atmosphere of glory such that the Syrophonician woman who insisted that *even dogs eat the crumbs from the children's table,* received her healing way before her time. She became an exception because in time, the cross had not occurred yet and salvation had not yet been made available to the gentiles. But she received her salvation and healing before its scheduled time according to God's calendar. Smith Wigglesworth, the man of God who raised the greatest number of people from the dead, understood this divine principle, hence he declared "*If the Holy Ghost does not move, I move the Holy Ghost*", meaning if the Spirit of God does not do certain divine tasks because it's not yet time for them to be released, I place a demand on Heavens for them to be released, whether it's time or not.

That is why the man who understand how to operate in the glory realm does not wait for the next six months the doctor has prescribed as time for him to receive his healing in the future, but he reaches up to the glory realm and possess his healing whether it's time or not. That is why when a healthy, bouncing baby boy is given birth within 3 months, humanity don't accept it but consider the baby to be premature because they don't understand the operation of the glory realm in which things happen way before their scheduled time. It might not be my earthly time for me to receive my breakthrough but my Heaven's time to receive. Hence, if I can't get what I want because the earthly time does not permit me to, I shift to the eternal realm, which is Heavens' time, and get it way before my earthy time. Do you want to become a millionaire and the world's richest? Don't wait until you are sixty to become one. Do you want move in miracles, signs and wonders manifested in raising the dead, opening the eyes of the blind and raising cripples form wheel chairs? Don't wait until you are ordained as a Bishop for you to start moving in power. Just tap into the glory ream and reach out to your miracle whether it's your time or not.

In view of this divine truth, the Bible also attests to the divine truth that *the lamb was slain before the foundation of time.* (Revelation 13:8). But how can Jesus be said to be crucified before even coming into the world? It's because long before Jesus came down to earth, in the realm of God, it was deemed as already completed. Although the inhabitants of the earth were waiting for the time for Jesus to enact the scenes by coming down to earth, and go through the cross, die and rise from the dead, in the realm of God, it was already a done deal because in God, the past, present and future are all in past tense. In other words, Jesus just went back in time into the foundations of the world where the stripes were already laid and enacted the scenes. This is to tell you that eternity breaks the law of time, gives you dominion over earthly time and ushers you into a dimension where you are able to touch the past, present and future as if they have already happened. That is why in the glory realm there is neither waiting, procrastination, postponement nor delays of any nature for things happen before their time.

In the absence of God's glory, the anointing is such a powerful way to minister to the congregation.

The reality is that when you minister under the anointing, the Holy Spirit uses your physical body to minister to the congregation such that when that anointing lifts off, the body is usually exhausted although you might not feel that physical drain or sudden experience of fatigue while the anointing is flowing. On the contrary, when you minister in the atmosphere of glory, you do it so effortlessly such that there are times when you just have to step aside and wait on the Lord because you cannot do anything under the weight of His presence. It is at that level of operation that you become a witness to the power of God as you watch and see the King of glory Himslef in action. During ministerial sessions, when the glory of God is moving powerfully, I have often stepped aside and relinquished my place to God and simply said, "*Holy Spirit, here I am. If you want me to do anything, just let me know*". This is a realm where people receive instantaneous healing and deliverance all over the congregation even without anybody praying for them.

The reality is that some people taste the spectacular experience of moving in the glory but then still want to crash back and minister under the anointing. Once you taste the glory, you may never want to go back to minister in the anointing again. However, this is not meant to dishonour the anointing in any way since it is such a great treasure of Heaven. What it simply means is that in the absence of God's glory, the anointing is such a powerful way to minister to the congregation but when the glory shows up in a meeting, the anointing gives way. When operating in the anointing, at times you can burn out. This is because the anointing of God is the outpouring for work. It's power for service. But operating in the glory of God is not the display of any gift. In the glory of God, you rest because energy is not being used. In the glory realm, it is all Him. Therefore, when we learn to live in the glory of God, our work becomes easy; from the outpouring to the glory, our lives are renewed.

The anointing can be measured in realms and dimensions but the glory is immeasurable and inexhaustible.

In the realm of the spirit, our levels of achievement are metered by the measure of the grace of God which is either the anointing or the dimension of the glory. However, it must be understood that the glory is not measured like the anointing. The anointing is a substitute substance for the glory. This means that you can substitute the glory for the anointing but you can never substitute the anointing for the glory because the operation of the glory is not subject to human control. It is therefore advisable that you operate under the anointing only when the glory of God does not show up but when it does, you can give way to God's sovereignty.

The truth is that the anointing could be measured. In 2 Kings 2, the Bible tells the story of the great prophet, Elijah, and how he was transported via a chariot of fire to Heaven. But before that time, Elisha, one of the prophets that served him entreated "*I pray thee, let a double portion of thy spirit be upon me*" (2 Kings 2:9). So, Elisha received a *double portion* of Elijah's spirit (2 Kings 2:9), which simply refers to a *double measure* of the anointing. As a result of that double measure of the anointing, the miracles recorded of his ministry exactly doubled those of Elijah. In essence, Elijah performed eight miracles while Elisha performed sixteen, which is exactly the *double measure* of what Elijah had accomplished in his life time. This record of an exact double portion of miracles in Elisha's life shows us that Elisha functioned in twice the power that Elijah had. This is the same principle by which God took the same Spirit that was upon Moses and imparted it upon the seventy elders (Numbers 11:17). In fact, it was said of Jesus by John that He had the Spirit upon Him without measure (John 3:34). The word '*measure*' being used here implies that the anointing had been previously given in measures to people in the Old Testament dispensation but now was given without measure to our Lord Jesus Christ.

Therefore, the term *double portion* refers to a mega or double dose of the anointing released for a massive supernatural harvest. It is a magnified or multiplied anointing given to individuals to accomplish tasks to greater or unimaginable proportions as compared to others. The term *double portion* does not mean something multiplied by itself; instead, it implies a measure of anointing that has been greatly enlarged, multiplied, increased exorbitantly in superfluous and measureless proportions. In essence, the *double portion* of the anointing is actually the mantle because a mantle is an anointing that has thickened as one graduate in a particular office. What Elisha called a "*double portion*" , we could term a"*double measure*" of the anointing to stand in the same office. The thing that was special about this anointing was the added dimension. It's the same anointing, except a different measure. What Elisha meant by requesting for a double portion was that he wanted a *double measure* of that anointing of God to stand in the office of prophet. That is why it is recorded that he did twice as many miracles as Elijah.

However, precaution must be taken regarding how we interpret the phrase, "*Double portion*" of one's spirit. This is because today, there are Christians who take a cue from Elisha and pray that the Lord would grant them "*a double portion*" of the anointing. That's a wrong prayer. The new creation doesn't require any double portion of the anointing because He's got all of it! When you were born again and the Holy Spirit came into your life, He didn't come in bits and fragments; He came to dwell in you in His fullness. What Elisha meant by "*double portion*" is understood from Moses' instruction to the Israelites about the rights of the firstborn in Deuteronomy 21:17: *"he shall acknowledge the son of the hated for the firstborn, by giving him a double portion of all that he hath: for he is the beginning of his strength; the right of the firstborn is his."* What this means is that, if for example, a man had six sons, he'd have to divide his entire inheritance into seven places, such that the firstborn gets a double share, as the right of the firstborn, while the remaining five sons get one each.

This was what Elisha requested for; the right of the firstborn. He wanted to assume the position of leadership amongst the other prophets in Israel, who at that time were under the tutelage of the prophet Elijah. And because of his spiritual perception, he got it and became the leading prophet over them (2 Kings 2:1-25). It's a misapprehension to say that Elisha wanted twice what Elijah had; there's no way that could have happened because it would mean Elisha asking Elijah for what he (Elijah) didn't have. Therefore, you don't have to ask God for a double portion of the Spirit, because the Bible says *"And of his fulness have all we received, and grace for grace"* (John 1:16). *For he whom God has sent speaks the words of God: for God gives not the Spirit by measure unto him* (John 3:34). Just as the Lord Jesus had the Spirit without measure, because He was sent of the Father, you also have the Spirit without measure (John 3:34) because Jesus said, *"As my Father hath sent me, even so send I you"* (John 20:21). So, all you need do is to continually get yourself filled with the glory to overflowing as the Apostle Paul admonished in Ephesians 5:18-19.

While we prophesy into the future when operating in the anointing, in the realm of glory, things happen the instant they are declared in the natural realm.

It is worth exploring the divine truth that contrary to operating in the realm of gifts and the anointing, in the glory, things happen the instant they are declared. You don't have to wait forver in order for something to be delivered to you. In view of this divine truth, let me explain the difference between *confession* and *declaration*. The word *confession* is originally derived from the Greek word, *"Homologous"*, which means to say exactly the same things as God says; If God says something should happen next year, it doesn't change, it remains next year; if He says you are going to receive a blessing after 10 years, it doesn't change, it remains 10 years according to earthly time. On the other hand, the word, *declare* comes from a Greek word *edere,* which means to bring something forward by either announcing, predicting or proclaiming it. That means you don't have to wait for it to happen. Instead, you make it happen within whichever time frame you decide to. You reach out into the future and bring it forth into the present such that it manifests now.

Therefore, in this *kairos* moment which marks the summation of ages and God's conclusion of His eternal plan for the earth, we need to move beyond the realm of *confession* to the realm of *prophetic declaration* so that we can secure things before their earthly time. The good news is that when operating in the glory realm, you don't have to wait for December to come. Why? Because when you declare a thing, you are bringing something forward that should occur in its natural time. In the Glory realm, there is no time. Time does not exist because the cloak is not ticking. Therefore, when operating in the realm of the Spirit, we must discern that time is virtually at an end, hence you don't have to wait until the end to believe God for the fulfilment of great things. That is why in Isaiah 46:10, God talks about, *"Declaring the end from the beginning, and from ancient times the things that are not yet done, saying, My counsel shall stand, and I will do all my pleasure."* This is to tell you that while the human mind is programmed to start something from the beginning and finish it at the end, God starts from the end and then comes back to the beginning to announce to us what He has already accomplished in the end. What an interestingly amazing God! And He does that for fun, for pleasure!

Therefore, when you begin flowing in the Glory of God, your level of faith begins to change. You learn that it is not necessarily the level of faith that brings the miracle when your faith brings you to the realm where things have already happened. It is not your faith that is trying to make something happen because you are in a realm where it already exits. Since we are still programmed to think according to time, we can miss something that truly is for now. I am not talking about a confession or how much faith you have because confession is simply agreeing with what God has said but declaration is altering that which God has determined to happen at a specific earthly time so that it can happen earlier according to Heaven's time. Do you know that there are times whereby you have to place a demand on the Heavens to release what you want and Heavens will not be left with any other choice except to release it? This is what Jesus meant when He said *whatever you release on earth shall be released in heaven*, meaning if you release something in Heaven, even way before its earthly time, it will be released. That is why when operating in the glory realm, we have to believe that no word that comes from the Throne is "next year".

Because the Heaven is the realm where it has already happened, it's not going to happen. Instead, it has already happened although in the earth it has not happened as yet. That is why you need to go beyond the realm of *confession* to the realm of *declaration* to bring forward that which is supposed to happen in the future, according to earthly time.

Philosophically speaking, the presence says God is here, the anointing says God has something in His hands but the Glory says IAM.

The presence is the multifaceted way that God shows up to meet us where we are. The presence is God with us. It is God inhabiting our praises (Psalms 22:3). The anointing is when God shows up in the presence and has something in His hands to give us. The anointing is associated with the hand of God but it is the presence that brings the anointing. It is not the other way around. The glory of God is His manifest presence, when God makes Himself visible to His people. When the men on the street can see God, they stand in awe of God for they have seen the glory. Things happen in the glory without us asking. That is why in this end time season, many people will be healed, delivered and even raised from the dead without a congregation, a song or an usher as the power of God invades the streets, market places and the public arena.

There is a new prophetic dimension surfacing in the glory realm whereby things are coming to pass as they are being said. In the glory realm, there is no procrastination, or delays because time is inconsequential. When God declared in an atmosphere of glory, *let there be light*, light came forth instantly. He didnt have to wait. Results came as words were declared. In the glory zone, there is no waiting because waiting is a process in time, of which we have dominion over time, we operate outside the time dimension because we were given birth to in the eternal realm which falls outside our time dimension. The reason why some believers experience delays in their lives is because of the absence of glory. The less you are filled with the glory, the longer it takes for you to cast out darkness and experience victory in your life. Real spiritual warfare takes place in the glory because there, the Lord fights for your battles. Outside the glory, you fight your own battles but inside the glory, God fights for you.

Notable is the realisation that even deliverance happens so fast in the glory zone because demons are not permitted to enter, death is rendered illegitimate and sickness is not permitted to reign. Because we have dominion over time, in the glory realm, you can declare a thing and use your royal prerogative to stipulate the time frame when that thing must come to pass, whether in a day, week or few hours. When the Bible says *you shall declare a thing and it shall be established for you*, it doesn't talk about flippantly declaring empty words in any direction but it talks about declaring things while in the glory realm or in an atmosphere of glory. That's when things happen. That is why those who function in higher reallms of glory don't wait for things to happen, instead, they make things happen.

It is much quicker to accomplish tasks under the glory than with the anointing.

It is worth exploring the divine truth that when the glory of God is fully realised, it ushers in a supernatural acceleration of the things of God. With this heightened degree of acceleration, comes a greater accomplishment of divine tasks, something that would not have been possible when solely operating under the anointing. The greater truth is that there is a heightened degree of acceleration in the realm of God's glory. Prophetically speaking, we are about to enter the eternal zone where time is loosing its grip on earth as eternity is invading time in the natural realm and the dominant realm, eternity, displaces time as the two worlds collide. As aforementioned, we are at the consummation of time when Heaven's atmosphere of glory is invading the earthly realm. This Heavenly atmosphere of bliss brings with it the eternal realm of glory, culminating in the manifestation of *Heaven on earth* and the rendering of the time dimension in the earthly realm inconsequential. In other words, we have entered *the rush hour* of God, a critical moment in God's calendar in which things are moving so fast in the realm of the spirit as we are adjourning quickly towards the second coming of the Lord, Jesus Christ.

In this critical *"Kairos"* moment, alarming breakthroughs in the realm of the spirit will be encountered in all extreme quarters of life. In other words, things which man never thought possible will be accomplished with the speed of lightning in this very hour. It has been scientifically proven that even the speed of light is slowing down as we are nearing the end of age. The Lord showed me recently in a divine encounter how time is running out and eternity is rushing in. It appears that we are encroaching towards a season when even time is even coming to a point of halt. Paul concurs that even *tongues are going to cease* (I Corinthians 13). Likewise, prophecy will also cease because everything is in the glory where there is no time. We are nearing the end of time, hence the time for prophecy to be fulfilled is narrowing. What would normally take 6 months is going to take a month. What would take a month is going to take a week. What would take a week is going to take a day. In just one week, God will allow you to do what would have taken fifty years to accomplish. This is to tell you how fast tasks are accomplished in the glory as opposed to operating in the anointing.

To cement this revelation with reference to scriptural evidence, the Bible records an incident in Luke 5:1-11, whereby Peter spent the whole night fishing but could not catch anything despite the fact that he was an experienced fisherman. Peter had previously received an impartation of the anointing from Jesus by virtue of his association with Him. However, he needed to be catapulted to the realm of glory to expedite or accelerate the process. That means the anointing to get the job done was present but the glory to perfect that anointing and speed up the process is what was lacking because in the glory, things are accomplished within the twinkling of an eye. However, when Peter received a divine instruction from Jesus to shift his position and cast into the deep and let down the nets for a catch, he exited the dimension of the anointing where he was operating using his own strength and stepped into the glory realm and instantaneously, he caught a multitude of fish within a split of a moment. This is because when the glory of God manifests, everything accelerates .

With the gifts of the spirit, we can reach individuals and with the anointing we can reach the multitudes but with the glory we can reach the whole world in a spilt of a moment.

The realm of glory is a higher dimension beyond the realm of gifts and the anointing, hence we need to tap into the realm of glory if ever we want to make a global impact. Prophetically speaking, that means millions of souls can be reached within a short period of time when operating under the glory than under the anointing. As a matter of fact, divine tasks which could have taken years to complete are accomplished within a flip of a moment in the glory. This is the reason why three thousand people were converted to Christ in one day when the Greater glory of God was extensively manifested during the days of the early church (Acts

2:41). The reality is that what could have taken a decade to build, with the anointing can be accomplished within a year or less when we consistently dwell in the glory. This is because time does not exist in the dimension of God's glory. That is why we can stand in the presence of God for hours and it seems like we were only there for thirty minutes.

The greater truth is that when the church operates in the dimension of glory, a spiritual acceleration takes place both in *quantity* and *quality*. In other words, there is a transformation that takes place evidenced by change in people's characters, drastic growth in ministry, alarming increase in finances, increased visitations to the Throne Room as well as an outburst of creative miracles. This tells me that when operating in the glory, everything accelerates and waiting time decreases. This is what happens when God is at work from a dimension that lacks the variables of time, space and matter. That means what used to take us a year to accomplish in the anointing will now take a day when operating in the glory. For example, if it normally takes a pastor five years under the anointing to build a two hundred member congregation, under the glory, it can take him one day to reach a thousand members. When operating in the atmosphere of glory, it is possible on the same day you start a ministry that you attain thousands of members. This happened at Pentecost whereby three thousand believers were added to the church as a result of the intense manifestation of the glory of God's spirit. With the glory of God, we can reach the whole world within a short space of time and witness and unprecedented avalanche of billions of souls into the Kingdom of God.

While the anointing is given to an individual for service to complete a specific task or assignment, the glory is given for elevation or promotion in the spirit.

Did you know that the glory is your divine credentials that qualify you to operate in the realm of the spirit? The glory comes as a result of one having successfully completed the delegated divine tasks and graduated to enter a higher spiritual realm. Hence, the anointing is what breeds the glory because the anointing causes one to execute tasks and brings them to perfect completion, which would then entitle one to be in a position to qualify to receive the glory. In other words, the anointing lays a ground or accentuates an avenue for the glory of God to be revealed. Remember that faith is the *first di-*

mension of the supernatural, the anointing is the *second dimension* and the glory is the *third dimension*. This implies that in order for one to operate and walk in the fullness of the glory, he should successfully operate in the anointing and foster a progressive application of the anointing so that he can graduate or be catapulted from the realm of the anointing into the realm of glory.

It is a greater truth that the anointing is given to bring the glory of God into manifestation. This is the ultimate purpose of the anointing in the kingdom. On the other hand, the glory is what establishes you in the realm of the spirit. The glory is your divine credentials that qualifies you to ascend to greater heights in the realm of God. When someone talks about being promoted to a higher position in the spirit realm, it's because they would have been elevated to a higher plane or realm of glory. This might not be the case in the realm of the anointing because the ministration of the anointing is still dependent on other factors, such as the character of the minister, the level of expectation of the recipients and the degree of consecration of the minister.

The anointing is the ability given to man by God to do whatever He has called him to do but the glory is God doing His work and operating according to His sovereignty and initiative.

It is worth unveiling the divine truth that the anointing operates according to human ability but the glory operates according to God's ability. God does everything by His glory and man does the work of God by His anointing. It is therefore stricter to operate in the glory than in the anointing because God demands that we move at the same pace, in the same direction and with the same perspective as Him when operating in the glory.

Mistakes for operating in the anointing can be overlooked but God demands accountability and judgement for any misconduct exhibited during the display of glory.

That is why it is very painful for man to be left behind when the cloud of God's glory has moved forward. The glory of God has moved to another location, leaving you clinging to the residue of His last visitation. It is therefore spiritually dangerous to stay behind where the glory or presence of God no longer manifests. Therefore, we need to keep pace with the glory of God and move at the same pace and in the same direction as the Spirit so that we stay relevant.

While the anointing is temporary as it comes and takes off depending on the nature of service, the glory takes a permanent abode or spiritual residence in humanity.

The major difference between the anointing and the glory is in longevity. The anointing comes upon a minister to enable him to perform certain ministerial tasks but once the glory of God comes, it takes a permanent abode in your spirit. Once an atmosphere of glory is present, it ushers a supernatural influence and divine arrangement of circumstances in the realm of the spirit that begins to attract favour, blessings, promotion, divine health, prosperity as it perambulates in the extreme quarters of your spirit. That is why the Bible declares in Philippians 4:19 that *the Lord supplies all our needs according to the riches in Christ glory*. That means all our needs, demands, prosperity and increase is regulated by the pre-eminence of glory. The glory is therefore the ultimate key to every prosperity, success, promotion and increase. It is a prerequisite for all dimensions of prosperity to be manifested. Hence, there is such a thing called *prosperity by the glory.*

What makes the glory permanent is that it's a supernatural substance that carries weight and has a long lasting effect in a human body.

Did you know that the glory of God is the heaviest *substance* in the universe in terms of weight and mass? That is why we talk of the heavy weight of God's glory. If energy is equal to matter or mass, then that means the glory of God, which is the supernatural power and energy is also matter and has weight, even though you can't see it. For instance, when you saturate a piece of cloth with the glory, substance and weight of God, it will be heavier than before it was saturated. In other words, it will have a greater weight that it did not have before. The object simply holds the same glory and then releases and transfers it when placed on someone by faith. That is why aprons and handkerchiefs were taken from the body of Paul and laid on the sick such that they were healed. Why? Because the glory of God carries weight and natural substances were used as a medium to carry that weight. This is also the reason why people fall under the power when they come into contact with the heavy weight of the glory of God.

The anointing and faith are governed by spiritual laws and principles but there is no law that governs the glory.

While we have the law of faith and the law of the anointing that prescribes specific principles to be followed or applied for these to manifest, there is no such thing as the law of glory. The glory is not governed by any law since it is administered directly by God himself. God created the laws for the universe and not for Himself, hence He is not accountable to any law. He did not create the law for Himself but for the purposes of governing the universe, hence His glory transcends all His laws. Operating in the dimension of glory therefore guarantees one success, greater power and greater manifestations because it is regulated directly from the Throne room of Heaven.

In the faith realm, the gifts never come to their maximum because the faith realm is the realm of susbstance. It is the realm of the beginning. That is why it is called *the first dimension.* However, in the glory, you see the maxcimum of the manifestation of the gifts of the Spirit. It is the higest level of operating in the realm of God. That is why it is called *the third dimension.* In the glory, it doesn't take two gifts to bring forth a manifestation. While in the faith realm it might take some time for gifts to reach full maturity, in the glory realm, there is no time period for growth. That's why when you get into the glory, miracles are instantaneous.

As believers, we can operate in the gifts of the spirit by faith and the anointing if we know the principles that activate them to operate. However the glory of God is the manifest presence which testifies of Heaven and the powers of the age to come.

It is worth exploring the divine truth that while in the past, more emphasis was placed on believers operating in the gifts of the spirit, there is a drastic transition from the realm of gifts (faith) to the realm of glory as God demands every believer to operate in the realm of glory in this end time season. While in the early days of revival, it was "*Just believe*", now its "*Just enter in*". That bypasses your struggle and the glory of God does the rest. Notable is the realisation that the glory of God operates according to God's sovereignty and initiative, not of man. He does whatever He wants, whenever He wants and in whichever manner He wants without depending on our faith, gifts or anointing. It is God doing His works without bringing in the participation of human beings. That is why the last move of God upon the earth will not come through a man or a woman but directly from God. Therefore, on the basis of the above revelation, a man knows he is in the dimension of glory when he does not operate in his personal measure of faith and the anointing. When one operates in the anointing, there is a tendency to feel physically exhausted because people place a demand on the anointing. However, operating in the glory automatically generates or produces more strength and power because of a direct divine connection with heaven hence, power flows directly from a perennial source of supply.

The truth is that the glory realm is a realm beyond the gifts and talents. Sadly, many believers today are majoring in the prophetic gift but not in the glory. Prophecy like any other gift, operates in the absence of glory but when the glory shows up, prophecy ceases as it is no longer needed as everything is revealed. That is why the best way to operate in the prophetic is in the presence of God's glory. This is what we call the *prophetic glory*. The prophetic glory is the Prophetic gifts intertwined with the glory. This is to tell you that although your prophecy may be accurate, the weight of the effect of your prophecy will depend on the level of glory of God in your life. A prophecy given in the glory has immediate and drastic life changing results. Jesus prophetically declared to a fig tree that it would die and at that moment it started to die. (Mark 11:12-14; 20-24). Prophecy is the means by which time is created. Revelation is the means by which time is known. Too many prophets today are putting into the future what God has already done and is available now. But the time has come that prophecy will no longer be about a future event waiting to come to pass. Instead, as the prophetic words are coming out of the mouths, that which we say will already be created and in motion before we finish speaking. Why? Because in the glory realm, there is no time for the clock is not ticking.

The glory of God's presence supersedes all gifts, anointing, faith or ministerial function although all these things come from Him.

It is a divine truth that God can heal, deliver and transform people during a service without the use of our faith or anointing but takes the initiative and works according to His will, hence the glory of God cannot be manufactured or faked. However, His glory can be attracted through worship. This means that you can never manufacture or produce the glory but you can attract, magnetise it and provoke it into manifestation. That is why we don't have to work very hard in order to bring the glory into manifestation. The reality is that many believers work hard to polish and perfect their gifts and anointing but in the glory there is not even an inch of hard work. Men work hard to graduate and perfect their gifts and anointing and that is what Paul advised in Philippians 2:12 when he said *that you must work out your own salvation with fear and trembling*. However, in the glory there is not even a kilo-joule of energy required.

Let me illustrate this with a quintessential example. In Exodus 19:8, the glory of God descended on Mount Sinai without the Israelites having to do anything. This is because the glory is not about you but God, while the anointing has everything to do with you. If the glory of God came as a result of us having to do something, then every day would be a revival because people are always fasting and praying. That is why man does not initiate revivals but every revival is initiated by God and driven by human beings. Therefore, the popular Christian cliché that men and women of God start revivals is a lesser truth. The greater truth is that God uses His sovereignty to initiate the greatest revivals on earth as stipulated in His calendar of times and seasons and then ignites the fire of passion in a man to bring it to accomplishment. In other words, human beings are just used as instruments to drive, spearhead and channel or direct the power of God is a particular direction in such a way that lives are changed and impacted.

On the basis of ample scriptural references, it is therefore evident that the experiences in the glory are profoundly different from those of operating under the anointing. By nature of operation, the anointing is the multiplying power of God. There is an anointing in every assignment God gives. For us to fulfil the divine destiny He has for us, it requires divine power. The Glory is the manifest presence of God releasing the power of God through the faith of God. The anointing is God's divine release while the glory is God's divine residence. In the anointing, Moses stretched forth the rod across the Red sea and it divided it but in the Glory, the shoes and clothes of the children of Israel did not wear out. In the anointing, David grabbed a lion and tore it apart with his bare hands but in the glory the appetite or metabolic system of the lion was altered when Daniel was thrown in a lion's den. In the anointing, Elijah earnestly prayed for rain to fall after three and a half years of drought but in the glory, water supernaturally appeared in a desert even without a sign of a cloud. The anointing is what God does through someone but the Glory is what God does without anybody. It is the Sovereign will of God moving in our midst. The atmosphere itself is charged by heaven. Through the blood of Jesus, we all have divine access to the throne of God. We can go there. But the gory is different. The Glory is when eternity comes to earth. It's when God chooses to arrive and appear to His people.

When operating in the realm of the anointing, you feel power coming out of you but in the glory you swim in the pool of God's power.

To illustrate this revelation with reference to a quintessential example from the word of God, when the woman with the flow of blood touched the hem of Jesus's garment, in response Jesus said *"Who touched me; for I perceive that power* (Dunamis) *has gone out of Me"* (Like 8:45-46). In other words, she made a withdrawal of the anointing upon Jesus. This is because it was God's power working through Jesus and people could place a demand and make a withdrawal of the anointing upon Him. Therefore, when the anointing is in operation, you feel virtue and power coming out of you as Christ did because there is a spiritual transaction that is effected by faith. According to the law of impartation, as people place a demand on the anointing or mantle of a man of God, they can receive whatever they desire. However, when we experience the glory, in His sovereignty, God chooses to work alone because the realm of glory is the realm of rest. Hence, we do not do anything, instead we just worship and bask in His presence. The glory of God works independently and is not influenced by any human action. More specifically, we work under the anointing but we rest in God's glory.

God will anoint you for everything He wants you to do but in the cloud of His glory, He will do His own works.

As aforementioned, the anointing is correspondingly to man, what the glory is to God. While we move, function and operate in the anointing, in the glory, God does His own work. However, in view of the above revelation, does it then mean that we should sit idle by with nothing to do and let the glory of God do everything? No! You mustn't sit and do nothing in hope that everything will automatically fall on your lap from the blue sky. At the same time, you must not haste and do everything by yourself. In a ministerial context, the secret is waiting on God to see if He chooses to manifest His glory and if He doesn't, then we can operate according to the anointing and spiritual gifts He has given us. We therefore need to strike a balance between *operating under the anointing* and *operating in the glory* since both of them are crucial in fulfilling God's plans and purpose in this end time season. In reality, there are certain things God has told us to do and anointed us to do hence, we should move forward in them if He doesn't take the initiative .

How then do I know whether I am moving in the anointing or in the glory?

People know that they are moving in the dimension of glory where they no longer need to use their faith or anointing. As long as you are still using your faith, you are still operating in the *first dimension* of the supernatural and as long as you are still operating in the anointing, you are still in the *second dimension.* You need to migrate or progress a step further to operate in the realm of glory, which is the *third dimension* of the supernatural. When you get to a point when you exhaust all your gifts and they cease to operate, it's an indication that you have entered into the realm of glory.

The anointing was given to heal the sick, but in the glory, we are covered with a supernatural immunity to sickness.

Did you know that in the atmosphere of glory, neither death, sickness nor any form of calamity or danger is permitted to prevail? This is because the same glory that operates on earth carries the same properties as that which originates in Heaven where there is no death or decay. Figuratively speaking, the anointing would shut the mouth of a lion but the glory changes the appetite and genetic make-up of a lion. Unknown to many people, it is actually the glory of God that changed the appetite of the lions when Daniel was thrown in a den of lion in (Daniel 6:16-24). It's not that the lions were not hungry that they could not devour him per se. Instead, it's the glory of God which filled the den that changed the whole metabolic or digestive system of lions.

The anointing can stop a lion from advancing in your direction but the glory changes the appetite and metabolism of a lion.

That is the reason why Adam could call or play with lions without them hurting him, because in the life of glory, there is neither danger nor calamity. The hunger pangs of a lion were activated the instant Adam sinned and lost the glory of God such that when they looked at Adam, they no longer saw their Master but a piece of meat that should be devoured. This is because in the atmosphere of glory, lions are herbivores but in the absence of glory, they are carnivorous. Likewise, the anointing was given to cut the head off of giants, but in the glory, giants don't even enter a territory at all.

The anointing operates in levels or measures but the glory operates in dimensions and degrees.

The glory enables us to reach nations, continents or the whole world because it is no longer faith, gifting or measure of anointing of man in operation. Instead, it is God himself doing the work. It is because the glory operates in dimensions. A spiritual dimension has greater coverage, as it consists of the width, length, depth and height. The Bible says in Ephesians 3:18 that *you being rooted and grounded in love, may be able to comprehend with all saints what is the width, length and depth and height of God's presence.* This speaks of the divergent realms and dimensions of operating in the glory. That means in the glory, we can explore deeper realms, depths and dimensions of God. That means the one who operates in the glory has a deeper experience of God than the one who operates in faith or anointing.

In Ezekiel 47:1-9, Ezekiel uses the physical phenomenon of water to demonstrate the various levels and degrees of the anointing. By so doing, Ezekiel's prophecy gives believers a clear picture of how the level of God's presence and power can increase in the lives of His people. In the context of this revelation, *water, streams and rivers* often refer to the presence and flow of God's Spirit. The highest attainable level of God's anointing is represented by the waters which flow from God's throne to individuals, groups or nations, and is often referred to as *the sea of the anointing.* Wherever these waters go, they bring healing and life to the needy. This implies that Spirit-filled believers have rivers of living water continuously flowing from their innermost being. Ezekiel gives a clear description of *a four-fold level of the anointing* upon every Spirit-filled believer, which is *the ankle deep anointing, knee deep anointing, waist deep anointing, overflow anointing or measureless anointing.* On the contrary, as much as there are different degrees of the glory of the sun, which is the *glory of sunrise, glory of sunshine and the glory of sunset*, there are also different degrees of the glory of God. There is the *first degree glory* which is an entry level, then there is a *second degree* which is a continuous progression into the realities of the glory realm and then there is the *third degree glory* which is highest realm of glory, which Paul described as a *far exceeding weight of glory.* However, the levels of the anointing cannot be equated to the *first, second and third* dimensions of glory, which is a higher plane of existence.

The realm of glory is timeless and holds greater creative power than the realm of the anointing.

In the anointing, when God speaks, we become impregnated with His word and as time passes, that word grows and develops, eventually causing us to give birth to that specific promise. However, when God's word is spoken in the realm of glory, the time it takes for the word to grow and mature is reduced to only a few moments; we see the promise instantly. This happens because the realm of glory is the timeless, eternal realm where God is. When God created Adam, he was timeless, ageless, eternal, and set into a timeless environment, which is God's glory. Man was not designed to be sick or to die, but to live in the glory of God, the realm of timelessness. Healings performed under the anointing might gradually happen over a period of time. However, miracles performed under the glory are instantaneous. That is why in the realm of glory, God causes our hair, teeth and fingernails to grow and our bodies to go through the natural progression of replenishing and replacing cells and this happens daily. An injury that would normally take weeks or months to be healed will be restored instantly when touched by God's glory. Time is actually made to serve those who know and understand their rights as citizens of heaven. When we experience the glory realm, we are experiencing timelessness.

The realm of glory holds the highest concentration of God's creative power than the anointing.

It is a divine truth that the glory carries the highest level of concentration of God's power. The Greek word to describe this spiritual phenomenon is, "*Epicaizo*". When coming into contact with God's glory, creative power can be released for creative miracles to take place. A creative miracle is not something broke being fixed, healed, or revived. A creative miracle is when something new is actually created in the place of the old. We've seen many creative miracles take place when the glory cloud manifests: new eyeballs, new eardrums, hearts recreated, legs grown out, and so forth. God wants to take you from glory to glory. If you are missing an organ, bone, flesh, or hair in any place on your body, God's glory is coming upon you now. If you have a limb shorter than the other, receive your miracle now. Any mental problems in your life or in your kids' lives, right now it is fixed in the name of Jesus. If you have lost your loved one and is lying on a death bed, in a coffin or at the mortuary, in the atmosphere of glory (*highest concentration of God's power*), command the dead to rise up and you will be thrilled at how the glory will quicken their spirit just like when Jesus commanded Lazarus to come forth.

Faith places a demand on the anointing of man but the glory places a demand on God Himself.

Where faith is exercised, it attracts anointing and pulls from the mantle; faith and anointing work together. When you go to a service, you pull from the mantle of the man of God. However, in the Glory, you make a pulling from God Himself. In other words, God introduces you to the glory Himself. In the realm of glory you are moving with the cloud, not the crowd. In the anointing, the man is seen. Unfortunately people look at the man as the one with the great anointing but when God uses humanity, people become mistaken and begin to idolize the man. In the glory, God demands to be seen Himself. Many people know how to stretch their hand to the mantle but don't know how to receive directly from God. We speak of *the cloud of glory* and the *rain of the Anointing*. The glory is like a cloud and the anointing is rain coming out of the cloud. The glory releases, produces or breeds the anointing. This means that the operation of the anointing is dependent on the glory.

The anointing was given to us to heal the sick, but in the glory of God, sickness is illegal.

There is a supernatural immunity that is given in the glory of God. The current church scenario is that multitudes are addicted to the anointing of man. Yes, the anointing is from God but you can come out of there and go directly to Him. In the anointing, Christ is our Healer. In the glory, He is our Creator. However, we need Him as both. In the anointing, we work. In the glory, we rest. In the anointing healings occur, but it's more on an individual level. For example, the minister may pray for someone and they're healed, then moving to the next, he prays, they're healed, and so on. The minster is operating in the healing anointing which covers him, and he releases it to the people. The cloud of glory however, is like a covering or a canopy that blankets the people and they all get touched at the same time. When the cloud of glory is present, there is direct contact with heaven hence revelation increases, the seer realm is opened, gifts are activated, and miracles happen all over the show.

Conclusively, it is therefore evident that the realm of glory is a higher dimension that operates on different spiritual principles as compared to that of the anointing. Hence, we should seek more of the glory than the anointing if ever we want to impact the world for Christ in this end time season. However, it must be expressly understood that although the glory supersedes the dimension of the anointing, that does not mean that the anointing is irrelevant. Both of them are required since they serve a specific purpose in the kingdom. The above revelation is given to help you migrate or graduate to a higher level which is the realm of glory. Both the anointing and the glory reveals, materializes and actualizes God's provisions and promises. They are the keys to integrating the spiritual kingdom of God with the natural life. There is no other way to materialize and actualize spiritual blessing outside the confinement or protocol of manifestation and revelation, which define how the anointing and the glory works.

HOW TO TRANSITION FROM THE REALM OF THE ANOINTING TO THE REALM OF GLORY

How do we step into the New Realms of Glory?

It is a typical scenario across a broad spectrum of Christian faith that many believers have had spiritual encounters and experiences in the anointing but a few have experienced the tangibility of God's glory. Due to reasons attributable to a lack of revelation, in some instances, many Biblical teachings in the church are centred around matters of faith, gifting and the anointing, but very little is said about the glory. The consequence of this divine phenomenon is that there is so much emphasis placed on faith and the anointing and less on the glory. This is a biased representation of spiritual truths, taking into account the reality that the Body of Christ is living on the edge as we have been ushered right into the very special moments of glory in the calendar of God.

However, it suffices to highlight that in this end time dispensation there is an alarming outcry and emphasis in the supernatural for a progressive transition from the realm of the anointing to the realm of God's glory . There is a paradigm shift and global migration from the substance of the anointing into the transcending higher realms of Glory. In essence, there is a drastic and profound transformation in the governance and administration of the anointing to the release of the glory in unfathomable ways never imagined before. While in the past decades there have been an emphasis for a transition from the realm of senses into the realm of faith and from the realm of faith into the realm of the anointing, now Heavens demands a further migration from the realm of the anointing into higher realms of glory. This is a major characteristic feature of the end time dispensation which shall see the masses being catapulted into higher realms of glory to experience what they have never seen, heard, conceived or experienced before. God wants to take us to newer, deeper and higher realms of glory we have never experienced before. In an endeavour to awaken this present generation to the reality of permanently moving, operating and functioning in the revelation of glory, God is raising a unique breed of ministers who shall actively drive, spearhead, rigorously participate or partake in the final move of God's glory and He is leading them on the path of transition from the anointing into the glory so that they can enter into the river of God's Shekinah.

In the current season across the body of Christ, there is a progression from the realm of the anointing and presence to the realm of Glory. In other words, more emphasis is placed on believers operating and tapping into higher realms of the glory than the anointing because the glory is a higher dimension of God's power as compared to the of the anointing. As a matter of fact, when Moses said to God, "*Please, show me your glory,*" he was actually implying that thank you for your anointing but I now want your glory. In other words, he had operated in the realm of anointing for quite some time and now he was expressing his readiness and wiliness to delve into a higher realm, which is that of glory. The statement which Moses uttered above shows a transition from the realm of anointing to glory by placing a demand in the spirit. Moreover, when Moses said to the Lord in Exodus 33:15, "*If you don't come with us, I'm not going*", he was so acclimatised to God's glory to such an extent that he could not do anything without the glory. That is why in the absence of God's glory, we can't do anything because the glory is the key and secret behind any dimension of miracles, signs and wonders which any believer can perform in this dispensation. It must therefore be expressly understood that life revolves around the glory as the source of all manifestations and this is the principal reason why I define life as *a constant migration, movement and operation in the dimension of glory.*

The reality is that there is a major transition occurring among us in this end time season as a result of an extraordinary move of God. Perhaps many people might sense it, perceive it or even feel the impact of its change. In some instances, you can't define it or label it but you sense the atmosphere is in transition. It is a Supernatural transition which marks the perfect timing in the calendar of God. It is a multiplying power within us, among us, and upon us. The church is transitioning to a different level, a deeper level of divine presence and power from one degree of radiant glory to another. We are moving from anointing to Glory, we are expecting a mighty wave of Glory to move us or plunge us deeper into His throne room in this season. In a practical sense, Moses moved from anointing to glory. Moses trekked up Mt. Sinai to commune with the Glory of the Lord. He'd seen the Glory at the burning bush but this was different. He'd moved in an Anointing when he confronted Pharaoh and delivered the Prophetic word to him but this was different. He'd moved in the anointing when He stretched out his rod and divided the Red Sea but this was different. It was an intense time in the glory of Jehovah. There, Moses received the divine norms for establishing the new nation of Israel.

In terms of efficiency, frequency and impact, this transition from the anointing to glory is like a person who moves from driving a car into driving an aeroplane. While both a car and a plane are means of transportation but the frequency, efficiency and speed with which they operate is totally different. By the same token while both the anointing and glory are aspects of God's power, the frequency of the glory, the level, depth, dimension and area of operation is much higher and greater as compared to the anointing. This revelation must propel your faith to move and tap into higher realms of awaiting glory. A car would stop at the robots, be intercepted by the road blocks, at times be hindered or delayed by the speed of other cars on the road. Contrary to how the anointing operates, the glory cannot be stopped; it does not operate on spiritual laws, hence cannot be hindered or delayed since it is the highest concentration of God's power.

This dispensation therefore marks the beginning of the season of divine exploration and discovery, to discover things in the supernatural that have never been experienced before. Increased visitations to the *throne room* shall therefore become a common experience as people are launched into the depths of God's presence to explore and unleash the fullness of His glory. The opening of the heavens to connect man with the release of the rain of glory shall consequentially result in many being elevated to greater heights in the supernatural. Therefore, in order for the body of Christ to access all these realms, it is highly imperative that we be sensitive to the transition that is taking place in the realm of the spirit.

THE SECRET TO TAPING INTO HIGHER REALMS OF GLORY

How do We Progressively Migrate into the Higher Realms of Glory?

A migration into any dimension or realm in the supernatural is always governed by revelation and a change in the application of spiritual laws and principles.

The Bible makes it clear that as far as operating in the glory is concerned, we are designed to move progressively from one realm of glory to a higher realm of glory (2 Corinthians 3:18). However, a migration into the dimension or realm of glory is always governed by the revelation and a change in the application of spiritual laws and principles. In view of the above, it is of paramount importance to highlight the fact that any migration or elevation from one level of the anointing to the other requires paying a price through undertaking intense sacrifices and strenuous spiritual exercises such as intense meditation on the word of God, persistent fasting as well as relentless prayer and practising the presence. And it happens that after advancing through various levels and dimensions of the anointing in the supernatural, one reaches a *breakthrough or ceiling point* beyond which he can no longer proceed further under reasonable circumstances. When this happens, this serves as an indication of one's readiness to make a transition from the anointing to the realm of glory. In other words, when you get to a level where you have operated so much in the anointing, to the extent that you have reached a ceiling point, then you are ready to break forth into a new realm of glory.

If a believer reaches a level of faith in the anointing in which nothing new is happening, then this is an indication that he is ready to enter the dimension of glory.

If an individual has reached a level of faith in the anointing whereby he has done everything in the Word but nothing new is happening, then this is a sign that one is ready to enter a new dimension of glory. Christianity is a life of progressive movement or migration from one level to the other hence believers are not supposed to operate at the same level of anointing or power for a long time. However, if you have managed to move in the power of God and tested all divergent depths and dimensions of the anointing but then nothing new seem to be coming your way, then that means the next level is to enter the realm of glory. I'm not talking about just siting and doing nothing and then waiting to enter the dimension of glory, but I'm talking about having exhausted all the dimensions of the anointing and stretched your faith to the limit of a breakthrough in the spirit. The Bible records an incident whereby Peter spent the whole night fishing but could not catch anything until Jesus stepped on the scene and ushered the glory of God and commanded him *to cast into the deep and let down the nets for a cash.* Peter was then convinced that it was time to change his career from that of fishing fish to that of fishing souls. It is important to note that one requires the right timing to migrate into higher realms of Glory. Prophetically speaking, you might have been labouring hard or migrating from one church to the other pursuing men of God or seeking after the anointing but when it's time to migrate to a higher realm of glory, Jesus will show up on the scene and you will be instantly catapulted into a higher realm of glory.

Transition into the realm of glory requires revelation knowledge for one cannot move into what has not been revealed to him.

Contrary to the unanimous view held by dozens of believers across a broad spectrum of Christian faith that a transition from one level of the anointing to the other requires undertaking certain spiritual exercises, transition into the realm of glory requires revelation knowledge for one cannot move into what has not been revealed to him .Without revelation, we can never see beyond the natural senses. The key that grants us access to the manifestation of glory in the natural realm is revelation since it can trigger or provoke a supernatural experience.

The level of revelation one has is directly proportional to the dimension of Glory one can be elevated into.

The greater truth is that God's glory must be revealed by the Spirit; it cannot be discovered by research or understood by reason. That is the reason why the church has been for long seeking the manifestation of glory without any success because they lacked the required revelation knowledge to manifest that glory. Hence, for the glory of God to manifest, it must be captured, received and recognised by our spirits through the revelation of the Spirit. Revelation is nothing more than the logics of God revealed to man for him to be able to think and operate out of eternity. Revelation elevates you above matter. You will never fully understand the present age until you understand the eternal age. Unless revelation comes, you have no access to the eternal. That is why we can't explain why there are some things that haven't happened yet unless God puts that faith in your spirit according to the revelation. Revelation precedes an impartation of faith. That is why faith comes by hearing the word of God. It's smooth sailing when the revelation comes and then faith abides. Revelation provides access to the highest realm of substance: the invisible. The name of the matter we cannot see is the substance from which God formulates things. This is what He has put resident in you. It is a five-letter word called *faith*. Faith is not a confession; it's what you have. It's a substance, matter and supernatural mass. The problem with us today is that we have diluted what the Bible calls faith and turned it into a cheap commodity. We have substituted alternatives for faith.

There are certain deep things of God that will never be known until they are revealed. This is the reality which Paul unveiled in 1 Corinthians 2:7 when he asserted that there are mysteries of God that are spoken in codes: *but we speak the wisdom of God in a mystery, even the hidden wisdom which God ordained before the world unto our glory*. Let me paraphrase it another way. If there is ever an hour the divine code are being decoded and revealed, it's now. I'm talking about the things of the spirit that are divinely coded and hidden to the natural man. There are manifestations of the spirit that are divinely coded. They don't happen for the sake of happening. In order for you to unlock these codes, you need to be catapulted into the higher realms of glory to access the secret pin and decode them in the natural realm.

A perennial hunger, unquenchable thirst and an insatiable appetite can catapult a believer into higher, deeper or newer realms of God's glory.

One key indication that portrays the church's readiness to migrate into higher realms of glory is a hunger, thirst and an insatiable appetite for the new revelation of God's glory. This forms the basis for *the law of desire* . It is a greater truth that in the realm of the spirit, things work according to people's desires. Your desire, passion and willingness to walk with God is what would provoke or trigger catapult-action into higher realms of glory. When Moses said to God, *"Please show me your glory"*, he was not just saying a general statement but he was expressing his deep desire for the supernatural glory and God unreservedly unveiled it to Him. Moreover, the Bible makes it clear that *the Lord shall grant the desires of your heart* (Psalms 47:4) but if you don't have any desires or hunger for the glory, what do you expect God to work with? A desire is like a flame of fire that ignites the glory of God in your spirit and set you ablaze, ready to move in signs and wonders. Therefore, a desire and hunger for the supernatural and to function in the heightened realm of the supernatural in signs and wonders is another indication that one is ready to embrace the realm of glory.

Spiritual readiness or preparedness is a prerequisite for one to enter into a higher dimension of glory.

Spiritual readiness or preparedness is another pre- requisite to taking a quantum leap into higher realms of glory. Whenever the glory of God shows up, it brings forth new spiritual encounters and experiences, unusual manifestations, creative miracles, signs and wonders, some of which might be peculiar or complex to understand. We must therefore be ready to deal with any manifestation lest we grieve the Spirit. There must not be any mistakes for operating in the glory to avoid side effects like Uzzah who mistakenly touched the ark of God and died (2 Samuel 6:7). A multitude of people have been restricted from entering a higher dimension of glory because they are not well prepared for that dimension. Preparedness for the glory entails rubbing thyself in His presence, fostering a heightened degree of intimacy with the Holy Ghost, provoking and building a glorious cloud of His presence by praying in other tongues as well as fervently and relentlessly staying in the Word of God. This is the essence of the law of preparation. If only you could do that, you can easily break into a new realm of glory. The Bible makes it clear that we grow from faith to faith, from glory to glory, and from one level of the anointing to the other. In other words, the life of a Christian is designed to progressively move in one direction – upward and forward only.

Openness and willingness for the progressive graduation from one dimension of the supernatural to the next.

It is the openness and willingness for the graduation and progressive migration from one level of faith to the other, from one level of anointing to another and from one level of glory to another that will catapult you to higher realms of glory. This entails a progressive – upwards and forward movement from the first dimension of the supernatural (*faith*) though the second dimension (*anointing*) until we reach the third dimension (*glory*). Lack of momentum and prowess can restrict or limit a man from operating in the realm of glory. This is because the dimension of glory requires a complete dependence on God. Therefore, anyone who is not willing to submit under the supremacy or pre-eminence or sovereignty of God is not ready for the realm of glory. It is bad theology, humanism and carnality that will prevent one from reaching higher dimensions of glory. Therefore, in your quest to attain higher realms of glory, you have to make an effort to align your attitude, character and mentality, to the will of God.

A progressive and exhaustive migration through the realms or the depths of the supernatural such as realm of faith, anointing, power, mantle and presence could also serve as an acid test and evidence that one is ready for the dimension of glory. Successfully rising up the ladder across these dimensions of the universe is also evidence that one is ready for the dimension of glory. The ability to pay a greater price to see the manifestation of Glory is therefore incontestable evidence that indicates one's readiness for higher realms of glory (Psalms 63:1- 2). The truth is that *faith* and the *anointing* works together. A person can exercise faith that puts a demand on the anointing of another believer. Faith attracts the anointing in that one places a demand of the anointing by faith. That is why there is such a thing as *faith in the anointing*. Likewise, faith also opens a doorway or passage for one to be catapulted into the realm of operating in the glory. That is why there is such a thing as *faith in the glory,* meaning *operating in the glory through faith.*

Progressive migration and development from one level of faith to the other.

There is an intricate connection between faith and the glory of God. Faith is the believer's spiritual antenna to hear beyond the natural dimension. Jesus said to Martha, in John 11:40, *"Did I not say to you that if you would believe you would see the glory of God?".* This implies that faith is a prerequisite for seeing the glory because having faith means you believe in what God can do. There is a difference between believing God for something using the measure of faith He has given you and God exercising His own God kind of faith. The realm of glory is the latter- God Himself in faith in action, what He believes and does on his own compared to what we believe based on our faith and anointing. While multitudes of believers attempt to operate directly in the glory, without the foundation of faith, it is highly advisable that believers first understand the dynamic operation of faith as a stepping stone to catapult you to higher realms of glory.

Faith's measure of rule is not the seen but the unseen. Faith openes to us the world, the realm and the zone that was before time. Faith affirms the invisible as its reality. Faith does not affirm the seen. Faith transcends the seen because it knows the seen is temporary. It supersedes reason. It supersedes your head and intellectualism. It supersedes the counterfeit because the counterfeit knows it isn't real. Do you remember that the Bible describes faith as *the substance of things hoped for and the evidence of things not seen*? Unknown to many believers, this is the basic, ordinary entry level of operating in the realm of faith. But when operating in the glory realm, even your level of faith changes. Faith stands on what has been predetermined by God, hence it imposes eternity into time. That is why time lines up with what God says you are and have now! It's not what time says, it's what God says. Therefore, when operating in the glory realm, hope is converted into evidence and evidence is converted into the substance and when it is converted into substance, it becomes time in the now. In a similar fashion in which deep calls unto deep, hope calls unto evidence; evidence calls unto substance and substance calls unto now. That is why in a deeper sense, faith is described as an invisible hand that reaches into the future to grab something and bring it into the present. Hope calls the beyond to here and now. Hope calls unto faith for its reality because it depends on faith for its structure, its embodiment. Hope is calling out for reality, coexistence and actuality. That's why when operating in the glory realm, you must have expectancy and act as if you know something is about to happen. Dance about it, shout about it and publicly declare it to the whole world and by so doing, you will be pulling it from its location in the future and bringing it into the present.

Transition from one realm of the anointing to the other.

There is an intricate connection between the anointing and the glory. If one continues to apply the anointing relentlessly, it is possible for him to be elevated or catapulted straight from the realm of the anointing into that of glory. The realm of the anointing is a lower place hence, moving into the realm of glory of like migrating from high school straight into tertiary. In the Old Testament, the glory of God fell on the terbanacle after the priests, the later and utensils had been anointed (Exodus 40). So, the anointing is the power of God working through us to do what He wants done on earth (glory). There are various degrees, levels and dimensions in the realm of the anointing. One level is equivalent to a step that must be taken or ascended as we progress in our ability to move in that anointing and grow spiritually in relation to it. No step can be skipped because each step represents essential aspect of maturity in spiritual matters. We must therefore go from step to step and from level to level without missing one until we reach a level at which we have fully developed the measure of the anointing we have received. When we reach the last level whereby we can do nothing further in terms of our anointing, then we have reached the fullness of that measure and stretched ourselves to the maximum limit. At this point, the only available option is to enter the realm of glory. However, many people have been taught that they can only move from faith to faith, glory to glory but they have not been exposed to the revelation that not only do we move within these dimensions of the supernatural but we can also move right across divergent realms of the supernatural, for instance from faith to the anointing and from anointing to the glory.

Ezekiel uses the physical phenomenon of water to demonstrate the various levels and degrees of the anointing. By so doing, Ezekiel's prophecy gives believers a clear picture of how the level of God's presence and power can increase in the lives of His people. Ezekiel gives a clear description of a five-fold level of the anointing upon every Spirit-filled believer. To cement this revelation with reference to a scriptural evidence Ezekiel gives us a narrative in which he says ,

"Afterward he (the man with a measuring line) brought me again unto the door of the house; and, behold, waters issued out from under the threshold of the house eastward: for the forefront of the house stood toward the east, and the waters came down from under from the right side of the house, at the south side of the altar. Then brought he me out of the way of the gate northward, and led me about the way without unto the utter gate by the way that looked eastward; and, behold, there ran out waters on the right side. And when the man that had the line in his hand went forth eastward, he measured a thousand cubits, and he brought me through the waters; the waters were to his ankles. Again he measured a thousand, and brought me through the waters; the waters were to the knees. Again the measured a thousand, and brought me through; the waters were to the loins. Afterward he measured a thousand; and it was a river that i could not pass over: for the waters were raised, waters to swim in, a river that could not be passed over (Ezekiel 47:1-9).

In the description of the anointing presented in the above mentioned scripture, Ezekiel reveals the **FOUR LEVELS** of spiritual maturity in the anointing. These are *ankle deep level, knee deep level, waste deep level and the overflow level.* By description, an ankle is the lowest part of a human body which can only take you to a certain point. By the same token, the *Ankle Deep level anointing* speaks of the first or initial level of the anointing that is released within a believer at the beginning of the Christian Life. In other words, at new birth as an individual receives Jesus Christ into his spirit, there is a measure of the anointing that is planted or deposited within him as he begins the Christian journey or walk. By the same token, the *Knee Deep level* of the anointing is not much greater than the ankle deep experience. However, it does indicate a deeper experience with God. The knee is slightly higher than the ankle and has the ability to bend and allow the body to perform diverse tasks. The knee is connected to prayer, hence this level represents entering into this second dimension of the anointing whereby Christians are learning to pray and develop a prayer life and dependence upon the power of God. The *Waist level* anointing often refers to influence, hence at this level, the believer is beginning to use the anointing to influence those who are in his sphere of contact. By description, the waist is a central part of the body which has the ability to influence or determine the direction of other parts of the body. At this level, a believer is active in the things of God and interacts with others around them. At *Overflow anointing*, the believer starts to produce the results of what the words of God talks about. In the same way a body is fully immersed at this level, believers operating at this level of anointing are fully immersed or deeper into the Spirit such that they are led by the Spirit. Therefore, this is a level of deeper miracles, deeper revelations, deeper faith and everything which believers do in executed in greater depth.

Moreover, this level of the *overflow anointing* is also a realm of supernatural manifestations and practical demonstrations of the Spirit and Power. This speaks of a *measureless anointing*. This is the level of the anointing at which Jesus operated or functioned under during His earthly ministry. The greater truth is that at this level of anointing, believers will do *greater works* than what Jesus did (John 14:12) because the Holy Spirit has now been sent without measure. It is at this level that the dead are raised, as there are mass resurrections experienced right across the body of Christ. Believers have developed a significant level of maturity in the anointing such that they are able to channel it in the right direction to impact the whole world. Therefore, the next level to break into after the measureless anointing is *the realm of glory*. The measureless anointing ushers you into the realm of glory in the same way a river in flood ushers water into the sea.

Ability to create an atmosphere of glory as evidenced by a cloud of His presence.

It is a divine truth that we are able to make a pull on the glory of God by staying long enough in His presence. The glory of God is given birth to in His presence. From a natural perspective rain does not come without the accumulation of clouds. Clouds represent the glory and rain represents His presence. Unless and until we have learnt how to build up an atmosphere of glory, we might not be able to make a pulling or withdrawal from it. It is therefore, highly recommended that believers build up an atmosphere of God's glory so that they can function in a realm of God's superabundance of glory. Building an atmosphere of God's glory is therefore such an imperative action if ever we have want to see the glory of God manifested like never before.

The question you are probably asking is: *How to we build an atmosphere of the glory cloud?* It's through prophetic declarations in the now. One of the principles of the spirit realm is that we must understand that the believer is God's agent on the earth who is authorised by God to declare the things of Heaven to earth. Heavens stands behind our words and agrees with it coming to pass (Mathew 16:19). To *declare* means to bring something forth. When you declare a thing, you are bringing something forward that should occur in its natural time. Just seeing it is not enough, declaring it and framing it causes it to stay framed. God wants us to declare in the realm of the spirit what we see in the Heavens. Faith believes and speaks it ahead of time. Time is not a determining factor anymore because in the realm of God, it doesn't exist. Until you speak, nothing is manufactured from the world beyond. One of the laws of mass that we were taught in science is that not all mass is visible. Faith is the invisible mass from which God creates the seen dimension. That is why it is the substance of things hoped for. Therefore until we speak, nothing is allowed to come from the world beyond without a revealed spoken word. Declaration gives permission or a license for things to be legally transacted from Heaven down to earth. It puts a stamp of Gods approval on any breakthrough or blessing to be released by the Heavens on earth.

Deepening of the realm of the miraculous or progressive demonstration of miracles, signs and wonders

It is a divine truth that a progressive and consistent demonstration or practical display of God's supernatural power through miracles, signs and wonders can delve one into a higher realm of glory. This is because as we demonstrate the power of God, we trigger or provoke the flow of the glory of God from within our spirits. This implies that the realm of the miraculous is the realm of glory because it is thorough the miraculous that the glory of God is revealed more and more. In some cases, it might happen that the glory of God is hidden or unknown to the masses. However, if a miracle such as raising one from the dead, is publicly performed, God's glory is revealed. That means the main purpose of miracles is to reveal the glory.

HOW TO ENTER THE NEXT LEVEL AND TAKE GLORY OF GOD TO THE EXTREME.

How do we practically enter Deeper and Unexplored Territories of the Glory Realm?

Prophetic declaration:

Prophetically declaring the new thing God has shown us is the first step. Without taking this initial step of obedience, the other steps are in vain. Elijah prophesied during a time of famine that the rains would come. (1 Kings 18: 1-2,41) Once God had spoken, the prophecy and declaration alone caused it to come forth. When we declare something under the direction of the Holy Spirit, that thing is being formed as we declare it. When you are in the glory zone and speak out what God is telling or showing you, things will start to be created at that very moment. Just as when God declared in Genesis 1:3, "*Let there be light*", a sound greater than a sonic boom ripping across time and space echoed through the universe such that light came forth instantaneously. When God tells you something while in the Glory zone, prophetically declare it and as you do this, God will send angels, people and circumstances to make the arrangements. Lack of prophetic declaration hinders the creation and birthing forth of those things into existence. We must mature to the stage where we declare what we see I the glory realm. Unknown to many believers, there are some things in the realm of the Spirit for which man declares the time frame, not God. To "*declare*" means to bring something forward. You don't have to wait for it to happen. Instead, you have to make it happen. You can bring it forth and it will manifest now. We lack the understanding of how to grasp these mysteries and bring them into our experience now. Prophetically speaking, there is a deposit, much like a bank account, in the Glory with your name on it. It is laid up for you in the Heavens. Accessing it is much easier than you would ever imagine. If we are trapped in this earth's time zone, then in one manner it is so. If we access the eternal realm, and begin to declare things, then we would be speaking from "up" to "down". If we have laid up treasure in Heaven, where our heart is, and where we have originated from, then why do you think it impossible to access the account you have there? God has already given us the compound interest rates of Heaven. They are up to one-hundred-fold return on our investment. Only when we tap into the glory realm are we be able to access these manifold blessings of heaven.

Prophetic Process and Intercession:

Between prophetic *declaration* and *manifestation*, you need to put yourself into a "*prophetic process*" called *intercession*, which is a birthing position in which you align your spirit to give birth to the prophetic word in the realm of the spirit. Intercession aligns our spirit and causes us to be rightly positioned in the spirit dimension so as to swiftly move, function and operate in the realm of the spirit. After declaring the word, we must enter into prayer or intercession so as to birth forth a manifestation in the physical realm. This was exemplified by Elijah who got down and put himself into a birthing position and prayed until it came (1 Kings 18:42). The prophecy is what gave life to it but the intercession is what caused it to grow until it was birthed forth. I'm reminded of what John Wesley, the great man of God once said, *"I pray for two hours every morning, that is if I don't have a lot to do. If I have a lot to do that day, I pray for three hours*". However, there are few things that need to be given divine correction pertaining to the ministry of intercession. Intercessory prayer is not a laundry list of requests. Intercession is not about making faithless, beggarly prayers as Heaven does not understand that kind of language. Intercession is not about pleading a cause and getting answers. We don't just get answers to our prayers - we become the answers because the world requires Heavens' solutions and not google answers. In other words, we gain knowledge and insight into solutions, hence we become a solution to the cries of millions across the globe.

Prophetic Perception:

Since it is a divine truth that in the realm of the spirit things are taken hold of through vision, imagination is such an integral aspect of possessing our possessions. Once you have interceded long enough to give birth to a manifestation in the spirit realm, the next step is to see those things that we have decreed in the spirit realm. This is what we call *Prophetic perception.* This is a spiritual sight necessary to see what God is doing in the invisible arena and in tandem with Him, you do exactly the same in the visible realm. It incorporates the ability to see the unseen, hear the unheard and then speak the unspeakable. This means that your imagination was intended by God to be the lens through which you apprehend the realms of spiritual realities. After intercessory prayer, Elijah started to look for the prophecy. He told his servant to look until he saw something – a cloud as small as a man's hand. And the minute he saw it, he got hold of the answer. This is because in the realm of the spirit, things are procured through vision. The instant you see, you take a hold of it.

Prophetic action:

Everything is perfected in the realm of the spirit when we demonstrate our actions of faith. According to the law of manifestation, in every action, there is a reaction. Actions of faith causes manifestations to be birthed forth in the natural realm as they send signals in the realm of the spirit alerting spiritual subjects of the legality of power being exercised. Therefore, the final step in tapping into the glory realm is prophetic action. Immediately after making a prophetic declaration, Elijah demonstrated his actions of faith when he began to run so as not to miss the next move of God. Strikingly, he girded up his loins and outran Ahab's chariot (1 Kings 18:43-46). Running was a prophetic action of faith that validated his declaration. Now, it's time to run, as the first signs have already appeared heralding the new outpouring. As Elijah did, gird up your lions and so as not to miss the next agenda of Heaven.

CHAPTER SEVEN

THE SEVENTH DIMENSION:

THE GOD DIMENSION: THE LOVE DIMENSION

The Law of Love

There is a realm which a man can be catapulted into which marks the highest level of spiritual contact with God. At that level of life, one is not chasing after any needs but rather after the heart of God. It is called the *seventh dimension*. That realm is the realm of love. It is a realm of perfection. It is a dimension in which God Himself lives, breathes and operates. That is a realm in which when catapulted into, man loses his own self-consciousness and begins to think as God thinks, talk as God talks, see as God sees and consequently view all things from God's perspective. In other words, in that realm, man begins to pour out the heart of God into every situation that he encounters. In that realm, everything is complete and perfect. Sickness, pain and death cannot operate in that realm. It is more powerful than any other dimension which man can ever function in this world. Did you know that the most powerful force in the universe is not the force of gravity or magnetic expulsion and repulsion but the energy of Love? When the Bible says that *we have been translated from the Kingdom of darkness into the Kingdom of light*, the word, "*translated*" in its original context in Greek connotes to some aggressive force that comes through love. Love can drag a man from the gravitational pull of hell and catapult him into the highest realm of God. Do you remember that Jesus said, *"If anyone wants to come to me, I will draw him to me"*. In this context, the word, *"Draw"* denotes the gravitation pull or energy of love that attracts, magnetises and lures sinners to the Kingdom of God. Love is therefore a force that can draw millions of souls into the kingdom of light and can also trigger an outbreak of the energy of the anointing through the tidal waves of the air and the torrential flow of the rain of God's power from the *Heaven's power house*, culminating in the greatest miracles ever performed in the history of mankind.

Now, the question is: How is this realm of love related to the raising of the dead? The *resurrection power* is a force of love – only the gravity or force of love can pull a man from the clutches of the worse demons of hell and set his soul free from torments. That is why any man who happens to operate in the realm of love and graduates into perfection, draws the power or divine energy that can cause the dead to jump out of the coffin even without saying a word. It is in this realm that Smith Wigglesworth would drag a dead body from a coffin, thrust it against the wall and then command it to walk. In case you thought love was a subtle, do you now see how aggressive the force of love is? That aggressive force that pulled the dead body from its coffin and commanded it to walk is actually the force of love. The Bible unveils the divine truth that Jesus raised Lazarus from the dead ***because He loved him*** (John 11:5). In other words, Jesus tapped into the realm of God's love and harnessed the divine energy that magnetised Lazarus's spirit from the spirit world and brought it back into its body. Since Lazarus was saved, it's apparent that his spirit was already in paradise but though the energy of love, Jesus managed to pull it back from Paradise into Lazarus's body in the natural realm. In essence, the bedrock of our Christian faith is the unmerited, fathomless marvel of the love of God exhibited by Jesus Christ on the cross at Calvary, a love men can never and shall never merit. That is why I say love is the most brutal force in the universe because it took love for Jesus to be brutally wounded and butchered on the cross, just to save humanity form sins. Only the force or energy of love can do that.

The greater truth is that the realm of love is a realm of God's glory. It marks the highest level of concentration of God's power. Therefore, if you wish to be mightily used by God in raising the dead as if you are waking people from sleep, it is highly imperative that you don't only operate in the dimension of faith but also in a higher realm of love, which is the *seventh dimension* of the supernatural realm. The Bible enumerates the most critical aspects of divinity which are *faith, hope* but then *love* is said to be the greatest (1 Corinthians 13:13). Why? Because it is a realm in which God Himself operates. God does not need faith or hope to operate but surely He requires love because He is love and love is a foundational pillar in His Kingdom. What actually distinguishes the realm of love from all other realms of God's power is that others can be counterfeited but no one can counterfeit love; it is impossible even for the devil himself to love. That is why the Bible says *if a man can pray in tongues of angles and has the ability to fathom all mysteries but does not have love, he is nothing* (1 Corinthians 1:13). Why? Because the realm of God is the realm of love, hence anybody who wishes to function in the greater depths of the miraculous should have the ingredient of love. God lives in love, He breathes love and speaks the language of love. Therefore, the realm of the miraculous is the realm of love. It is therefore worth mentioning that only those who would manage to tap into the realm of love will be launched into greater depths of raising the dead because this realm is sacred, hence can only be entrusted to those who have stood a test of love.

THE AUTHOR'S PROFILE

Frequency Revelator is an apostle, called by God through His grace to minister the Gospel of the Lord Jesus Christ to all the nations of the world. He is a television minister, lecturer and gifted author, whose writings are Holy Ghost breathings that unveil consistent streams of fresh revelations straight from the Throne Room of Heaven. He is the president, founder and vision bearer of Frequency Revelator Ministries (FRM), a worldwide multiracial ministry that encompasses a myriad of movements with divine visions such as Resurrection Embassy (*The Global Church*), Christ Resurrection Movement (CRM) (*a Global movement for raising the dead*), the Global Apostolic & Prophetic Network (GAP) (a *Network of apostles, prophets and fivefold ministers across the globe*), Revival For Southern Africa (REFOSA) (*a Regional power-packed vision for Southern Africa*) and the Global Destiny Publishing House (GDP) (*the Ministry's publishing company*). The primary vision of this global ministry is to propagate the resurrection power of Christ from the Throne Room of Heaven to the extreme ends of the world and to launch the world into the greater depths of the miraculous. It is for this reason that Frequency Revelator Ministries (FRM) drives divergent apostolic and prophetic ministry visions and spiritual programmes such as the Global School of Resurrection (GSR), Global Resurrection Centre (GRC), the Global Healing Centre (GHC), Global School of Miracles, Signs and Wonders (SMSW), Global School of Kingdom Millionaires (SKM), Global Campus Ministry as well as Resurrection Conferences, Seminars and Training Centers. To fulfil its global mandate of soul winning, the ministry spearheads the Heavens' Broadcasting Commission (HBC) on television, a strategic ministerial initiative that broadcasts ministry programmes via the Dead Raising Channel *(a.k.a Resurrection TV)* and other Christian Television networks around the world.

Presiding over a global network of apostolic and prophetic visions, Apostle Frequency Revelator considers universities, colleges, high schools and other centers of learning as critical in fulfilling God's purpose and reaching the world for Christ, especially in this end-time season. As a Signs and Wonders Movement, the ministry hosts training sessions at the Global School of

Resurrection (GSR) which includes but not limited to, impartation and activation of the gifts of the Spirit, prophetic declaration and ministration, invocations of open visions, angelic encounters and Throne Room visitations, revelational teachings, coaching and mentorship as well as Holy Ghost ministerial training sessions on how to practically raise the dead. This global ministry is therefore characterized by a deep revelation of God's word accompanied by a practical demonstration of God's power through miracles, signs and wonders manifested in raising cripples from wheel chairs, opening the eyes of the blind, unlocking the speech of the dumb, blasting off the ears of the deaf and raising the dead, as a manifestation of the finished works of the cross by the Lord Jesus Christ. The ministry is also punctuated with a plethora of manifestations of the wealth of Heaven through miracle money, coupled with the golden rain of gold dust, silver stones, supernatural oil and a torrent of creative miracles such as the development of the original blue print of body parts on bodily territories where they previously did not exist, germination of hair on bald heads, weight loss and gain, as well as instantaneous healings from HIV/AIDS, cancer, diabetes and every manner of sickness and disease which doctors have declared as incurable.

The author has written a collection of 21 anointed books, which include *The Realm of Power to Raise the Dead, How to become a Kingdom Millionaire, Deeper Revelations of The Anointing, Practical Demonstrations of The Anointing, How to Operate in the Realm of the Miraculous, The Realm of Glory, Unveiling the Mystery of Miracle Money, New Revelations of Faith, A Divine Revelation of the Supernatural Realm, The Prophetic Move of the Holy Spirit in the Contemporary Global Arena, The Ministry of Angels in the World Today, Kingdom Spiritual Laws and Principles, Divine Rights and Privileges of a Believer, Keys to Unlocking the Supernatural, The Prophetic Dimension, The Dynamics of God's Word, The Practice of God's Presence, Times of Refreshing and Restoration, The Power of Praying in the Throne Room, The End Time Revelations of Jesus Christ and Rain of Revelations,* which is a daily devotional concordance comprising a yearly record of 365 fresh revelations straight from the Throne Room of God.

Apostle Frequency Revelator resides in South Africa and he is a graduate of Fort Hare University, where his ministry took off. However, as a global minister, his ministry incorporates prophecy, deliverance and miracle healing crusades in the United Kingdom (UK), Southern Africa, India, Australia, USA, Canada and a dense network of ministry visions that covers the rest of the world. As a custodian of God's resurrection power, the apostle has been given a divine mandate from Heaven to raise a new breed of Apostles,

Prophets, Pastors, Evangelists, Teachers, Kingdom Millionaires and Miracle Workers (*Dead raisers*) who shall propagate the world with the gospel of the Lord Jesus Christ and practically demonstrate His resurrection power through miracles, signs and wonders manifested in raising people from the dead, thereby launching the world in to the greater depths of the miraculous. To that effect, a conducive platform is therefore enacted for global impartation, mentorship, training and equipping ministers of the gospel for the work of ministry. Notable is the realization that the ministry ushers a new wave of signs and wonders that catapults the Body of Christ into higher realms of glory in which raising the dead is a common occurrence and demonstrating the viscosity of the glory of God in a visible and tangible manner is the order of the day. Having been mightily used by God to raise the dead, in this book, Apostle Frequency Revelator presents a practical model of how one can tap into the realm of God's resurrection power to raise the dead, impact the nations of the world and usher an unprecedented avalanche of billions of souls into the Kingdom, Glory to Jesus! May His Name be gloried, praised and honored forever more!

AUTHOR'S CONTACT INFORMATION

To know more about the ministry of Apostle Frequency Revelator, his publications, revelational teachings, global seminars, ministry schools, ministry products and Global missions, contact:

Apostle Frequency Revelator

@ Resurrection Embassy

(The Global Church)

Powered by Christ Resurrection Movement (CRM)

(Contact us in South Africa, United Kingdom, USA, Germany, Canada, Australia, India, Holland & Other nations of the world).

As a Global Vision, The Ministry of Apostle Frequency Revelator is present in all the continents of the World. You may contact us from any part of the world so that we can refer you to the Resident Ministry Pastors and Associates in respective nations.

Our offices and those of the ministry's publishing company (Global Destiny Publishing House (GDP House), are ready to dispatch any books requested from any part of the world.

Email:
frequency.revelator@gmail.com

Cell phone:

+27622436745
+27797921646/ +27785416006

Website:
www.globaldestinypublishers.co.za

Social Media Contacts:

The Author is also accessible on Social media via Facebook, twitter, instagram, YouTube, and other latest forms of social networks, as Apostle Frequency Revelator. For direct communication with the Apostle, you may invite him on Facebook and read his daily posts. You may also watch Apostle Frequency Revelator on the Dead Raising Channel a.k.a Resurrection TV and other Christian Television channels in your area.

Christian products:

You may also purchase DVDs, CDs, MP3s and possibly order all of the 21 anointed books published by Apostle Frequency Revelator, either as hard cover books or e-books. E-books are available on amazon.com, Baines & Nobles, create space, Kalahari.net and other e-book sites. You may also buy them directly from the author@ www.gdphouse.co.za. You may also request a collection of all powerful, revelational teachings by Apostle Frequency Revelator and we will promptly deliver them to you.

Ministry Networks & Partnerships:

If you want to partner with Apostle Frequency Revelator in executing this Global vision, partnership is available through divergent apostolic and prophetic ministry visions and spiritual programmes such as the Global School of Resurrection (GSR), Christ Resurrection Movement (CRM), Resurrection TV (a.k.a The Dead Raising Channel), the Global Apostolic & Prophetic Network (GAP), Global Resurrection Centre (GRC), the Global Healing Centre (GHC), Global School of Miracles, Signs and Wonders (SMSW), School of Kingdom Millionaires (SKM), Global Campus Ministry and other avenues. By partnering with Apostle Frequency Revelator, you are in a way joining hands with God's vision and thus setting yourself up for a life of increase, acceleration and superabundance.

GLOBAL MISSIONS, PARTNERSHIPS & COLLABORATIONS:

If it happens that you are catapulted into a higher realm of the supernatural following the reading of this book, please share your testimony with Apostle Frequency Revelator at the contacts above, so that you can strengthen other believers' faith in God all around the world. Your testimony will also be included in the next edition of this book.

If you want to invite Apostle Frequency Revelator to your church, city or community to come and spearhead Resurrection Seminars, Conferences, Dead Raising Training Sessions or conduct a Global School of Resurrection (GSR), whether in (Europe, Australia, Canada, USA, South America, Asia or Africa), you are welcome to do so.

If you want to start a Resurrection Centre or establish the Global School of Resurrection (GSR) in your church, city or community under this movement, you are also welcome to do so. We will be more than willing to send Copies of this book to whichever continent you live.

If you want your church or ministry to be part of the Christ Resurrection Movement (CRM) and join the bandwagon of raising the dead all around the world, you are welcome to be part of this Heaven-ordained commission.

If you want more copies of this book so that you can use them in your church for seminars, teachings, conferences, cell groups and global distribution, please don't hesitate to contact Apostle Frequency Revelator so that he can send the copies to whichever continent you are. Upon completion of this book, you may also visit www.amazon.com and under the "Book Review Section," write a brief review, commenting on how this book has impacted your life. This is meant to encourage readership by other believers all around the world.

If you want to donate or give freely to advance this global vision, you may also do so via our ministry website (www.globaldestinypublishers.co.za) or contact us at the details provided above. If you need a spiritual covering, impartation or mentorship for your Church or ministry as led by the Holy Spirit, you are welcome to contact us and join the league of dead-raising pastors that we are already mentoring in all continents of the world.

If you have a burning message that you would like to share with the whole world and you would want Apostle Frequency Revelator to help you turn your divine ideas and revelations into script and publish your first book, don't hesitate to contact us and submit a draft of your manuscript at the Global Destiny Publishing House (www.globaldestinypublishers.co.za). We will thoroughly polish your script and turn it into an amazing book filled with Throne Room revelations that will impact millions across the globe, glory to Jesus!

The Lord Jesus Christ is coming back soon!

Made in the USA
Columbia, SC
01 August 2021

42797215R00087